YESTERDAY & TODAY ™

THE AUTO EDITORS OF CONSUMER GUIDE®

Publications International, Ltd.

ISBN-13: 978-1-60553-338-4
ISBN-10: 1-60553-338-6

Manufactured in China.

8 7 6 5 4 3 2 1

Library of Congress Control Number: 2010925873

Credits

Photography:

The editors would like to thank the following people and organizations for supplying the photography that made this book possible. They are listed below, along with page number(s) of their photos.

Scott Baxter: 111; Ken Beebee: 24, 123; Les Bidrawn: 38, 146; Jeff Cohn: 99, 131, Back cover; Brian Czobat, autostock: 131; Thomas Glatch: 26, 38, 52, 105, 140, 148; Gary Greene: 27, 69; Sam Griffith: 18, 95; Jerry Heasley: 39, 120; Don Heiny: 25, 58, 77, 135; Brandon Hemphill: 19; Christopher Hiltz: 11, 21, 51, 103, 123, 152; Bud Juneau: 43; Milton Kieft: 12, Back cover; Lloyd Koenig: 137; Dan Lyons: 45; Vince Manocchi: 10, 12, 13, 15, 20, 21, 37, 38, 40, 42, 43, 49, 54, 61, 66, 75, 85, 87, 89, 105, 107, 108, 114, 138, 142, 148, 149, 150, 151, 153, Back cover; Jeff Markley: 133; Roger Mattingly: 99; Doug Mitchel: 20, 46, 47, 48, 55, 61, 87, 93, 97, 108, 109, 110, 115, 121, 125, 127, 147; Mike Mueller: 53, 58, 87, 104, 112; David Newhardt: 86; Bob Nicholson: 112; Thomas R. Rigg: 61; Roger Servick, Syd Mead, Incorporated: 101; Tom Shaw: 76; William J. Shintz: 134; Steve Statham: 51; Richard Szczepanski: 64; David Temple: 18, 19, 139; Bob Tenney: 71; Phil Toy: 40, 53, 106; 20th Century-Fox Film Corporation: 44; W. C. Waymack: 15, 18, 22, 41, 53, 55, 62, 67, 70, 90, 122, 139, 141; Phil Wedlake: 113; Nicky Wright: 12, 90, 91, 136

Owners:

Special thanks to the owners of the vehicles and collectibles featured in this book for their cooperation.

John B. Albert: 41; Art Astor: 49, Back cover; John Baker Sr.: 45; George Ball: 15; Richard Bayer: 38; Karl Benefiel: 148, Back cover; David Berlew: 58; Gary Blakeslee: 46; Glen Bohannan: 149; Ken Boorsma: 64; Dick Calarossi: 42; Kim Cardin: 53; Bob & Brad Chandler: 104; John Chandler: 38; Chicago Car Exchange: 18; Joseph & Lauretta Chromicz: 48; Gregg Cly's Mustang Muscle & More: 51; Debbie Colariro: 134; Dr. Randy & Freda Cooper: 85; Dells Auto Museum: 148; Keith Devereux: 108; Kim Dobbins: 10; David Domash: 107; J. Glenn Dowd: 71; Ralph Dowling: 25; Richard Drake: 153; Evan Eberlin: 53; Ron Edwards: 147; Jim Elijah: 108; David & Karen Erschen: 55; Finn Fahey: 153; Clarence E. Ferguson: 91; Robert M. Forker: 67;

Bob Fruehe: 10; Jack & Jan Garris: 55; Gregory Gates: 75; George & Tony Gloriosa: 93; Alden Graber: 121; Buzz Gunnarson: 37; Dean Hammond: 135; Shel Harriman: 12; Rick Harris: 139; Russel Hoeksema: 76; Houston Police Department: 137; Tom Howard: 21; Robert M. Huff: 141; Illinois State Police: 133; John Infinger: 87; Gary L. Ingersoll: 20; Edward R. Keshen: 47; Darrell Kombrink: 90; Leroy Lasiter: 90; Norman Lenstrom: 113; Douglas Lombardo: 125; Los Angeles County Sheriff's Department: 142; Robert C. Lowry: 70; Anthony Lucarz: 127; The William Lyon Collection: 13, 40; Frank Mandile: 77; Vince Manocchi: 66; Larry Martin: 22; H. M. Martins: 150; Bruce Meyer: 86, 87; Diane & Steve Mierz: 77; Bruce Miller: 53; Amos Minter: 120; Motorcar Portfolio: 19; Jim Mueller: 58; Dick Nelson: 19; Bob Newman: 105; W. R. "Rick" Parsley: 149; David Patterson: 39; Richard Perez: 151; John W. Petras: 109; Bob Peterson: 112; Steven Pierce: 138; Arnie C. Postier Jr.: 112; Glen & Joyce Pykiet: 62; Jim Reily: 127; Mark A. Rice: 54; Carl M. Riggins: 38, 146; Jim Russel: 18; David Sanborn: 13; Darryl Scheleger, MD: 87; Schmerler Ford: 95; Robert J. Secondi: 110; Rob & Dottie Sharkey: 108; The Donald Sikora II collection: 11, 21, 51, 103, 123, 152; Don Simpkin: 61; Alan Simpson: 40; Stan Sokol: 12; Jerry C. Spear: 150; Frank Spittle: 24, 123; Bill & Collette Stanley: 48; Rick Stroh: 27, 69; Neil Swartz: 105; Tommy Taylor: 139; Dwight A. Tschantz: 12, Back cover; Charles & Mark Vandervelde: 111; Mike Venarde: 89; John P. Vetter: 26, 52, 140; Larry & Beverly Wake: 122; Brent Walker: 106; Tom & Thelma Walters: 18; Dr. Irv Warren: 43; John & Connie Waugh: 75; Dan Weiss: 20; John White & Bill Knudson: 43; Jerry Windle: 136; Gary & Monica Wise: 15

Our appreciation to the historical archives and media services groups at Ford Motor Company.

About the Auto Editors of Consumer Guide®:

For more than 40 years, Consumer Guide® has been a trusted provider of new-car buying information.

The Consumer Guide® staff drives and evaluates more than 200 vehicles annually.

Consumerguide.com is one of the Web's most popular automotive resources, visited by roughly three million shoppers monthly.

The Auto Editors of Consumer Guide® also publish the award-winning bimonthly *Collectible Automobile®* magazine.

Contents

Foreword

Welcome to *Ford: Yesterday & Today*™, a colorful tribute to what many regard as the most significant name in automotive history. As the pioneer of mass-produced vehicles, Dearborn-based Ford literally put the world on wheels, creating the auto industry we know today and changing the lives of billions. And to think it all started more than a century ago with a farm-bred Michigan tinkerer who once declared "History is bunk."

Henry Ford's simple homespun demeanor belied a complex personality. He could be engaging, free-thinking, and public-spirited, but also grumpy, closed-minded, and bigoted. Blessed with innate mechanical gifts and a shrewd head for business, he conceived the landmark Model T as a simple, rugged little car that could be easily fixed and driven most anywhere at a time when mechanics and paved roads didn't exist outside major cities. But his true genius was in developing the mass-production techniques and material resources that allowed selling the Tin Lizzie in ever greater numbers at ever lower prices. Public response was predictably enormous, and Ford Motor Company was soon America's biggest automaker by far, its founder one of the world's richest, most influential industrialists.

As time passed, however, Henry became ever more eccentric, and the company suffered for it. He refused to retire the Model T even when demand waned, then inexplicably gambled everything on the 1928 Model A, which, fortunately for him, was a big hit. He then conjured America's first low-priced V-8 car, but only to one-up pesky six-cylinder competition. He resisted "modern" features like hydraulic brakes, yet pursued dubious ideas like making car bodies from soybeans. He named son Edsel as company president in 1919, but consistently usurped his authority. Even before Edsel died in 1943, Dearborn had dropped to third in industry sales and earnings, behind General Motors and Chrysler. When the old man himself finally succumbed, in 1947, Ford was in utter disarray, its future uncertain.

It was left to Edsel's son, Henry Ford II, and some brainy "Whiz Kids" to secure Ford's future. That they did. Helped by a boom market born of soaring post-World War II prosperity, Dearborn soon reclaimed title as America's number-two automaker. Though Lincoln, acquired in 1922, and Mercury, established in 1939, played a role, the recovery was owed almost entirely to the Ford brand, which steadily closed the sales gap with chart-topping Chevrolet—and occasionally outsold its perennial GM foe—thanks to ever faster and flashier cars and trucks.

Ford achieved even greater success in the 1960s, starting with the highly popular Falcon compact, then with America's first midsize car, the Fairlane. Ford also prospered with handsome "standard" cars and ever more elaborate "personal luxury" Thunderbirds. But its biggest triumph was the Mustang, a jaunty, affordable "ponycar" that was perfectly in tune with the think-young spirit of the times. Ford also captured the country's imagination with its "Total Performance" program, an all-out assault on motorsports from NASCAR to drag racing to international long-distance events. This effort not only spurred showroom sales but inspired a squadron of exciting driver-oriented street machines. These, too, have long been highly prized collectibles.

Everything changed in the 1970s, when Ford and its Detroit rivals were forced to deal with a suddenly sober public mood and stricter government standards for passenger safety, tailpipe emissions, and—after an unprecedented gas crunch—fuel economy. Many buyers, newly disillusioned with American cars, embraced a rising tide of Japanese-brand imports that not only offered better mpg but superior build quality. These trends continued into the 1980s, aggravated by the sharp recessions that bookended that decade. Even so, the Blue Oval recovered market strength with striking "aerodynamic" cars like the 1986 Taurus and increased demand for its F-Series trucks, now the nation's top-selling vehicles of any kind. Adding the Explorer sport-utility vehicle helped Ford to achieve record sales and profits in the truck-crazy market of the 1990s.

Detroit has since struggled against a host of life-threatening problems, many of its own making, and to cope with a new century's vastly altered geopolitical realities. But while GM and Chrysler were finally forced to accept government aid in 2009, Ford managed to avoid the taint of bankruptcy to the benefit of sales, profits, and public confidence. Though predictions are always risky, Ford's future now seems brighter than it has been for a very long time, a happy ending for a book that we hope you'll enjoy.

The Auto Editors of Consumer Guide®
Lincolnwood, Illinois
April 2010

CHAPTER ONE

Family Favorites

The story of the Ford Motor Company, not to mention the cars and trucks it has made, closely relates to an American family: the Fords. Henry Ford was born in Dearborn, Michigan, on July 30, 1863. His son, Edsel, another central character in the story of the company, was born in November 1893. A month later, Henry built his first experimental gasoline engine. The Ford Motor Company incorporated on June, 16, 1903; it was the third automobile company organized to produce Henry Ford's designs. Though he dabbled with racing cars starting in 1901, an early dream was to create the $500 "family horse," and Henry preferred to produce lighter, more affordable cars. Ford's ninth distinct model, the Model T of 1908, proved to be the automobile that put America on wheels. In more recent years, the company would offer an increasing variety of products, but the least exciting, yet most practical, family cars would serve as the backbone of Ford's product line.

Early station wagons were called "depot hacks" because they often served resorts by collecting visitors from the train station. By the time this 1956 Ranch Wagon was made, they were popular family cars, particularly in the fast-growing suburbs.

It was on October 1, 1908, just about a month before William Howard Taft was elected President of the United States, that the Ford Motor Company, then barely five years old, unveiled the machine that many historians think of as the most significant automobile of all time. Henry Ford called it the Model T. It was only built as an open touring car at first, but within a few months, other body styles were added to the line. Strictly a utilitarian vehicle, the Ford took no beauty prizes, and it won no speed contests. Still, its 22-horsepower 4-cylinder engine could propel the Model T to a top speed between 35 and 40 miles per hour,

Top left: Early Model Ts, like this 1909 touring car, were available in colors, all-black didn't come until 1914. **Top:** The Model T used a 4-cylinder engine. **Above:** Ford added a closed model, the centerdoor sedan, for 1915. The picture is of a 1919 model, note the door centered on the side of the body. **Left:** The "Tudor" model debuted for 1923. Note the forward-mounted doors.

As COOL in summer, as it is snug and weatherproof in winter, the Ford Closed Car has an unfailing appeal to women and children, who appreciate its many features of comfort.

Furnishings and equipment of the Sedan are of the highest order, including soft,

durable cushions, revolving type window lifts, windshield visor, cowl ventilator, rugs, dome light, door locks, electric starting and lighting equipment.

And the Ford Closed Car costs so little to own and operate that mother and children can use it daily for every errand of business or pleasure.

TUDOR SEDAN, $590   FORDOR SEDAN, $685   COUPE, $525   (All prices f. o. b. Detroit)

Ford
CLOSED CARS

adequate for the era's mostly unpaved roads. Widely known as the "Tin Lizzie," the Ford became the butt of a thousand jokes. But it was this machine, more than all the others combined, that was responsible for putting America—and the world—on wheels. On the strength of the Model T, Ford's yearly production increased from 10,000 in 1908 to nearly two million 15 years later. As early as 1913, Ford outproduced all other American automakers combined. The formula for the Model T's success was basic: It was simple, it was tough, and it was cheap, but not cheaply built. The first Model T sold for $825, but the price was steadily reduced as output increased. By 1924, a brand-new Ford could be purchased for as little as $260. When the final T was built in 1927, more than 15 million had been produced.

Top left: By the time this advertisement ran in 1924, the marketing of the increasingly affordable Model T attempted to portray the vehicle not as a luxury, but as part of a normal middle-class lifestyle. Ford pitched its cars as empowering the common man, or woman. **Above:** Ford often used scale models of its products as promotional devices. In the 1960s, the company offered several $\frac{1}{25}$-scale plastic model kits of historically significant Fords. This five-inch-long 1925 Model T appeared around 1964. It was manufactured for Ford by AMT. **Left:** Henry Ford was born on a Dearborn, Michigan, farm on July 30, 1863. He died in Dearborn on April 7, 1947.

Above: The Model A replaced the long-lived Model T for 1928. This 1929 Fordor sedan listed for $625. **Top right:** Ford pulled off a publicity coup in 1932 when it introduced a V-8 engine to the low-priced field. This V-8-powered Fordor wears fancy DeLuxe trim. **Far right:** Ford's "flathead" V-8 debuted on March 31, 1932. The 221-cubic-inch engine made 65 horsepower. **Right:** A 1932 five-passenger Victoria coupe.

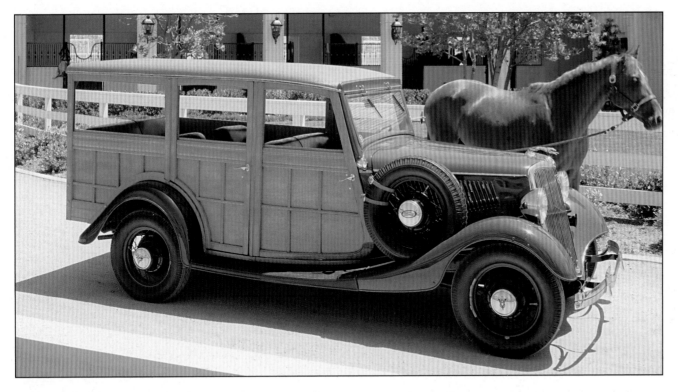

The suspense built for months, ever since the announcement was made that Ford would replace the Model T with a brand-new car. When the Model A finally made its debut, on December 2, 1927, its introduction literally created more excitement than any similar event in the history of the automobile. It was estimated that in the United States alone, more than 10 million people flocked to showrooms to inspect the new car. The Model A was bigger than its predecessor, and the new four-cylinder engine developed 40 horsepower, nearly double the Model T's rating. In addition, the new car was handsome. Henry Ford cared little about styling, but son Edsel did. The Model A's appearance resembled the then-current Lincoln, a monument to Edsel's good taste. The next big changes arrived for 1932 and included the first V-8 engine in the low-price class, the legendary "flathead." An improved version of the Model A's four was also offered. Styling was spectacular, but it was only used for one year as streamlining began to influence Ford styling in 1933.

The Universal Car

ONE name comes quickly to mind when you think of "The Universal Car." The description is distinctively Ford. No other car is used by so many millions of men and women in every part of the world. Everywhere it is the symbol of faithful service. . . . That has always been a Ford fundamental. Something new is constantly being added in the way of extra value. Each year the Ford has widened its appeal by increasing its usefulness to motorists. . . . Today's Ford V-8 is more than ever "The Universal Car" because it encircles the needs of more people than any other Ford ever built. It reaches out and up into new fields because it has everything you need in a modern automobile. . . . The Ford V-8 combines fine-car performance, comfort, safety, beauty and convenience with low first cost and low cost of operation and up-keep. There is no other car like it in quality and price.

Top left: Wood-bodied station wagons were rather low-production offerings when this 1934 "woodie" was built. Sales for this model were 2905, nearly double 1933's tally. **Top, above center:** Buyers of 1935 DeLuxe Tudor and Fordor sedans could, for the first time, choose between the traditional "flatback" model, or this new "trunkback" style. **Above:** Choosing the new trunk added $20 to the selling price. **Left:** Sensational new looks, improved ride, and important mechanical improvements helped make the 1935 Model 48 the best-selling car in America.

We do hope your new Ford arrives by daylight!

DE LUXE FORD V-8

Above: In this 1939 advertisement, the stylish DeLuxe model takes center stage, with the Standard appearing only in the secondary illustration. **Above right:** Though ready to shift over to war production, Ford assembly lines produced cars at a normal pace in 1940. Here, alignment of headlamps is checked on a Standard Tudor. **Right:** This 1941 Tudor is from the new top-line Super DeLuxe series.

The 1939-40 Fords had their origins in the 1935 models, but the streamlined look came off much better. With the 1938 models and continuing through 1940, Ford began the curious practice of making the last year's DeLuxe model (slightly modified) the Standard series and creating a new DeLuxe series. The '39 DeLuxe was a smart looking job influenced by the new 1939 Mercury, and stylist Bob Gregorie and his crew carried Ford streamlining to its highest form with the '40 DeLuxe. Engineering advances included hydraulic brakes for 1939 and industry-standard sealed-beam headlamps the following year. There was a new, bigger Ford for 1941. A three-piece grille, chubby-looking bodies, and sleek profiles were

distinguishing features. Traditional Ford underpinnings were retained: beam front axle, transverse springs, torque-tube drive, and flathead V-8. One addition was a new available six-cylinder engine. The '42s were mildly facelifted, but soon after the December 7, 1941, attack on Pearl Harbor, World War II halted civilian production until July 1945. During the war, Edsel Ford passed away, and in time his son, Henry II, became president of the company. The 1946 Ford looked nearly identical to the '42 model on the outside, but the bigger 239.4-cubic-inch flathead previously fitted to Mercurys came under the hood of V-8 models. During 1947, the cars were freshened a bit and continued unchanged through 1948.

Above: The '49 Ford Custom Fordor started at $1559 and attracted more than 248,000 buyers. **Above right:** Like the Model T, the 1949 Ford—here a Custom Club Coupe—was one of the most important cars in Ford history. The styling was well-received from day one. Sales took off, and more than 1.1 million were built during the long model year. It was Ford's best tally since 1930. **Opposite top left:** The woody station wagon was the most elegant in the line. **Opposite top far right:** Changes were subtle for 1950. **Opposite bottom:** A 1951 Ford V-8 participated in that year's Mobilgas Economy Run, a test of endurance and frugality held in the desert southwest. Even with Ford-O-Matic, a V-8 could return 18 mpg.

Ford's first redesigned postwar cars debuted for the 1949 model year. They were new inside and out—underneath, transverse "buggy springs" were dropped in favor of independent front suspension and rear parallel leaf springs. Modern slab-sided fenders were a clear departure from the bulbous fenders of previous years. A "propeller spinner" centered between horizontal grille bars highlighted front-end styling. A "6" or "8" in the center of the grille spinner indicated the 226-cubic-inch inline flathead six or 239-cubic-inch flathead V-8, both carryover engines. After the revolutionary 1949 redesign, Fords received only minor updates for 1950. A new "dual-spinner" grille was the most visible of 1951's changes, but the big news was Ford's first automatic transmission, the Ford-O-Matic.

Left: All-steel station wagons were new to Ford for 1952. There were three in all: a new two-door Mainline Ranch Wagon, a four-door six-passenger Country Sedan (shown) in the Customline group, and the Country Squire in the top-shelf Crestline series. **Top:** This '53 Country Squire shows off the model's simulated wood trim. **Above:** Ford produced 305,433 Customline Tudor sedans for '53. **Bottom left:** The 1954 Ranch Wagon started at $2029. **Below:** There was big news under the hood in '54 as the 22-year-old flathead was retired in favor of a new overhead-valve V-8 called the "Y-block." It displaced 239.4 cubic inches and was good for 130 horsepower.

Top left: Fords looked dramatically new for 1955. Flashy "checkmark" bodyside trim identified the new Fairlane series, which replaced Crestline as the poshest Ford. **Top right:** A smart, subtle facelift graced 1956 Fords with a wide-crate grille and horizontal parking lights in wraparound chrome pods. This Mainline Tudor sedan wears a single option: two-tone paint. **Above:** The Country Sedan was the best selling '56 Ford wagon with 85,374 deliveries.

Ford cars received their second full restyle in three years for 1952. Round taillights, a one-piece windshield, and discreet rear fender bulges were visual highlights of the new body design, while a new "K-bar" frame helped improve overall rigidity. The model lineup was revamped to include base Mainline, Customline, and top-end Crestline trim levels. underhood, the big news was a peppy new "Mileage Maker" six that put out 101 horsepower. To keep pace, the trusty flathead V-8 received a 10 horse hop-up, boosting its output to 110 ponies. The basic design lasted through 1954, but that year a modern overhead-valve V-8 engine was added to the mix, along with a new ball-joint front suspension. An extensive facelift of the 1952 design arrived for 1955 and was so skillfully executed the cars seemed all new. In 1956, Ford tried to make safety a selling point.

Nineteen fifty-seven was a vintage year for Detroit. For Ford, it was a watershed. The '57 line was broad with 20 different models spread over two wheelbases for the first time in postwar Ford history—not counting Thunderbird of course. Low-end Customs, and mid-grade Custom 300s, along with all wagons, rode a 116-inch wheelbase. Fairlanes and new range-topping Fairlane 500s used a 118-inch span. Except for the engines, the '57s were new from the ground up. Despite the low, squatty design, they were every bit as roomy as the 1955-56 models, but wider doors made entry and exit even easier. Styling was attractive, and production hit a record 1.67 million units for the model year. A economic recession in 1958, along with a poorly received facelift, helped drop 1958 output to less than 950,000 units.

Top left: Automakers test cars in extreme temperatures, as evidenced by this frozen '57 Ford. **Above:** Side trim on Custom 300s, like this Tudor sedan, was similar to that used on the Fairlane 500, but it sat lower on the body. The tailfins were more subdued than the Fairlanes as well. **Left:** In addition to the basic Ranch Wagon, Ford offered this flashier Del Rio in 1957.

Top left: For a two-door sedan, the 1957 Fairlane 500 Club Sedan offered a lot of flash for $2281. **Above:** The 1958 Custom 300 Tudor looked clumsier than the '57. Quad headlights were an industry fad at the time. **Left:** Country Sedans were popular vacation cars for many American families. **Below:** This hardcover book, the *Ford Treasury of Station Wagon Living, Volume 2* was published in 1958. Contents included reports on camping equipment, sections on campgrounds in the U.S. and Canada, and vacationing tips. Not surprisingly, Ford wagons are featured throughout.

Right: This cab driver is making good use of the 1959 Ford's larger trunk. **Below:** Midyear, a Thunderbird-inspired Galaxie series was added. The Victoria hardtop sedan started at $2654. **Bottom right:** Ford showed off this unusual concept called the Pushbutton Camper based on a 1959 Country Squire. A campsite on wheels, all the gear deployed at the press of a button from the driver's seat.

the long, sophisticated line

that flows

through Ford

styling

has become

the
silver
curve of
success

Galaxie
by Ford

The long, elegant silver curve now moving over the American Road on hundreds of thousands of 1960 Fords has become the hallmark of success. To its last beautifully proportioned inch, this is the decisive style of the decade, a direction-pointer as certain as a compass needle.

The Galaxie is a clear-cut expression of the newest Ford styling trend—the uniquely formal roof balancing beautifully on the graceful sweep of its long, sophisticated body. Here, in Ford, you find distinctive automotive luxury at its finest . . . the first fashion of the station in America's best-selling car—the car with the silver curve of success.

For 1959, Ford grafted new outer body panels and changed much of the 1957-58 inner structure to create what it immodestly billed as "The World's Most Beautifully Proportioned Cars." The claim was debatable to be sure, but the new squared-off look was considered handsome at the time. It was downright conservative next to the wild "batwing" '59 Chevy, and Ford ended up winning the annual sales race. The first full-size Ford of the Sixties looked like a completely different car inside and out, but it actually was another of the company's famous camouflage jobs that gave the appearance of being a much newer car than it actually was. The fresh look didn't sit well with shoppers though, and sales were down by about half a million units. In other big news for 1960, Ford's compact Falcon debuted.

Above: Galaxie returned for 1960. It still sat atop the full-size Ford line and used a unique roof line. This Town Sedan was the top seller in the series with 104,784 delivered. **Right:** Sedans in Ford's other three series used this roof stamping. Note the wraparound rear window on this Fairlane 500 Town Sedan.

Right: The 1961 Fairlane Town Sedan sold better than 96,000 copies. **Below:** Galaxies, like this Club Sedan, wore extra trim including ribbed stone guards behind the rear wheels. **Below center:** Save the wagons, all full-size '62 Fords were Galaxies. This sedan is a top-line Galaxie 500. **Bottom right:** In December 1961, Ford purchased Philco, a maker of radios, televisions, and home appliances. Some of Philco's 1962 offerings are shown.

Ford returned to more traditional styling for 1961. Again, it was an extensive facelift; much of the inner structure was carried over, but all of the sheetmetal below the windows was changed. The familiar round Ford taillights reappeared, with an aluminum plate between them repeating the front grille pattern on top models. The rear batwings from 1960 were eliminated, allowing for a full-width trunklid. The tiny fins at the rear were similar in size and style to those seen on the 1957-58 models, only now they were integrated into the door handles. Bodies for 1962 were very similar to those of '61, with enough trim and panel changes to make buyers think otherwise. The most obvious change was the clipping of the vestigial fins, keeping with an industry trend. Other changes included new roof panels and a flatter grille. Ford's compact Falcon was a sales success, and for 1962 Dearborn decided to split the difference between it and the full-size models and add a third model. The result was the Fairlane, the industry's first true intermediate.

Right and far right: Essentially an enlarged Falcon, the 1962 Fairlane fell between Ford's compact and the Galaxie in both price and size. Ford's new small-block V-8 debuted as Fairlane's optional engine. **Below:** A Fairlane wagon was added for 1963, here in faux "woody" Squire trim.

The greatest auto show ever assembled under one dealer's banner is at your Ford Dealer's! For '63 there are four complete lines of fine cars from Ford! 44 different models, including the first **FALCON** convertible! The brand-new **FORD FAIRLANE** wagons and hardtops! The new Super-Torque **FORD GALAXIE!** The most luxurious **THUNDERBIRD** ever! Turn the page and start the fun.

Ford skillfully freshened the full-size line again in 1963 and 1964. Though some of the basic design went back to the 1957 model, the constant updates kept the cars looking new. The 1965 models were the most changed Fords since 1949, if not the most changed in the company's history. They were truly new from the ground up and used coil-spring suspension front and rear. Other big news for 1965 was the introduction of posh LTD two- and four-door hardtops at the top of the Galaxie 500 range. With yearly updates, the basic car served through the 1968 model year. The full-size Fords were completely redesigned for 1969 with new bodies and a chassis of new design. The '69 full-sizers were promoted as being wider, longer, and quieter than the cars they replaced.

Classic

Son of Classic

FORD

Since 1929 when Ford invented the mass-produced station wagon, Ford wagons have been the standard of quality...the prime innovators year after year. A quick test drive in any one of thirteen Ford models tells why Fords outsell every other wagon made. Even apart from the unique Magic Doorgate (swings down for cargo, swings open for people) these '66 Fords are classics. Best-selling. Best of Breed!

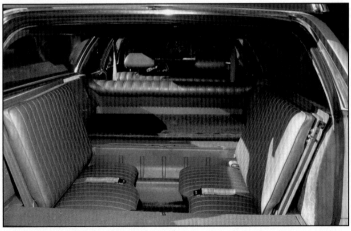

Opposite far left: This 1963 catalog claimed Fords were the liveliest cars of the year. **Opposite top:** For '63, big Fords, including this Country Sedan, were thoroughly restyled. **Opposite bottom:** The '64 Galaxie 500 four-door wore a new roofline. **This page, top left:** This Custom two-door was the most affordable full-size 1965 Ford, at $2313 to start. **Top right:** This 1966 ad compared the new Country Squire to the classic '46 woody. **Above left:** The big 1969 Fords were new stem to stern on a 121-inch wheelbase. The Country Squire continued as Ford's luxury wagon. **Above:** Center-facing rear seats allowed this Squire to seat up to ten.

Right: Full-size 1971 Fords featured a new front end. The heavy bumper and prominent center grille defined a styling theme that Ford's big cars wore for years to come. **Below:** Buyers demanded more and more luxury touches on cars as the Seventies progressed. This 1975 Gran Torino Brougham stickered for $4837.

Full-size cars remained family staples as Ford entered the Seventies, and in 1971 the company sold nearly a million of its big cars. Intermediates were gaining popularity though, and when Ford released its redesigned Torino for 1972—the Fairlane name was retired after '70—buyers snapped up nearly half a million of them. Full-size models sold poorly in the wake of the 1973-74 energy crisis but regained popularity to a degree as time passed. Still, smaller, better trimmed cars made significant gains with family shoppers. Ford tried a luxury compact with the 1975 Granada and discovered sales gold. A new family of Fairmont compacts arrived for '78, riding on a versatile chassis that over time underpinned many Ford products. Following GM's successful downsizing of its big cars for 1977, Ford did the same for '79.

Left: Ford president Lee Iacocca stands next to a 1975 Granada, the company's new "luxury" compact. **Bottom left:** Replacing the compact Maverick, the 1978 Fairmont line included two- and four-door sedans, plus a station wagon. **Below:** Ford downsized its big LTDs for 1979. **Bottom right:** For 1983, the LTD name switched to a midsize car based on Fairmont mechanicals. A 1985 sedan is shown.

Left: The 1986 Taurus was a very daring departure for a midsize American sedan. Buyers took home more than 236,000 of them the first year. **Above:** The 1986 Taurus line also included a stylish wagon. **Below:** Ford's last full-size wagon was this 1991 Crown Victoria Country Squire LX. The basic design dated to the 1979 LTD.

For 1986, Ford replaced the junior LTD with the front-drive Taurus. These four-door sedans and wagons represented Ford's strongest-ever claim to Detroit design leadership: clean, smooth, and carefully detailed, yet not lumpy like some "aero" cars. With ultramodern styling, good performance, and value prices, Taurus charged up the sales charts. Taurus was updated for 1992 and promptly became America's best-selling car. It was redesigned for 1996, but then lost the sales crown and never got it back. The big rear-drive Crown Victorias were still available, but the circa-1979 design wasn't changed much until 1992 when the wagon was dropped. The big rear-driver was rebodied again in '98 and then saw few changes past 2010. Another family-friendly large Ford sedan, the Five Hundred, arrived in 2005 with front- and all-wheel drive.

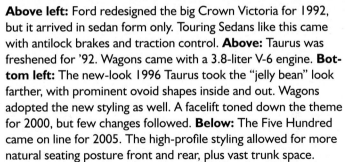

Above left: Ford redesigned the big Crown Victoria for 1992, but it arrived in sedan form only. Touring Sedans like this came with antilock brakes and traction control. **Above:** Taurus was freshened for '92. Wagons came with a 3.8-liter V-6 engine. **Bottom left:** The new-look 1996 Taurus took the "jelly bean" look farther, with prominent ovoid shapes inside and out. Wagons adopted the new styling as well. A facelift toned down the theme for 2000, but few changes followed. **Below:** The Five Hundred came on line for 2005. The high-profile styling allowed for more natural seating posture front and rear, plus vast trunk space.

Above: Taurus took over from Five Hundred for 2008. **Right:** The 2006 Fusion was hard to miss with its bold three-bar grille. **Below:** Station wagons are no longer fashionable, so the 2008 Taurus X tried to hide its car-based mechanicals and look like a sport utility vehicle.

The Five Hundred was bigger than a traditional midsize sedan, so Ford went after the sweet spot of the market with the 2006 Fusion. A 2.3-liter four and a 3.0-liter V-6 were the engine choices for this front-drive sedan. Buyer response was tepid to the Five Hundred, so when it was facelifted for 2008 it also gained a name that the company hoped would jump start sales: Taurus. Similarly, the Five Hundred-based SUV, the Freestyle, became Taurus X. Fusion and Taurus were both impressively reworked for the 2010 model year, and when the new versions debuted in 2009 the American new-car market was suffering the effects of a deep recession.

Top left, top, and above: Fusion received substantial upgrades for 2010 and arrived in the midst of the worst new-car sales market in memory. Fusion's impressive new hybrid model paired a 2.5-liter four-cylinder engine and an electric motor. The "SmartGauge" digital instrumentation assists efficient driving. **Left:** The 2010 Taurus benefited from a major makeover, with revised interior and exterior styling. A 3.5-liter V-6 and a six-speed automatic were standard.

CHAPTER TWO

Sunshine Specials

In the earliest days of the Ford Motor Company, all of its products were open models. Ford's first closed body style arrived by 1908, but open models still dominated. For the first dozen years or so of the company's existence, Ford made many millions of open-top automobiles, but, strictly speaking, they were not convertibles. Roadsters and touring cars populated the company's order sheets, but those cars don't meet the commonly held definition of a convertible. To qualify as a convertible, a car's top must be permanently attached to framework that folds down. Also, a true convertible has a fixed windshield and roll-up side windows. The first Ford to generally meet this definition was the 1915 Model T Couplet. By the Thirties, Ford sold more convertibles than any competitor. Until the Thunderbird went on sale for 1955, all Ford convertibles were standard-size models, but in the Sixties, convertible choices expanded into compact and intermediate sizes, along with the sporty Mustang. Today, only the latter survives.

Right: New slab-sided styling induced 51,133 admirers to select a 1949 Ford convertible. Sold only in fancy Custom trim and with V-8 power, this was the most popular Ford convertible yet.

Top: A circa 1906 Ford Model N drives past Ford's Piquette Avenue plant in Detroit. Ford built the plant in 1904 to replace a much smaller facility the company rented on Mack Avenue. Here, the first Model T was built in the fall of 1908. **Right:** Ford introduced this new Model T Open Roadster, or Runabout, for 1911. A similar model, the Torpedo, included doors.

Ford's first factory was a rented plant on Mack Avenue in Detroit. The young firm built a new factory in 1904 on Detroit's Piquette Avenue, but quickly outgrew the 67,000-square-foot facility. By January 1910, Ford's new "Crystal Palace" factory in nearby Highland Park, Michigan, began cranking out Model Ts. Though Ford listed a closed coupe version of the Model T as early as 1908, throughout this era open body styles dominated the offerings and the sales charts. When Model T production ended in 1927, two open body styles—the Runabout and the Touring—were Ford's best-sellers.

Above left: With a fixed windshield frame, retractable glass side windows, and a form-fitting fabric top, the 1915 Model T Couplet was a precursor to the modern convertible. **Above:** The 1916 Couplet was given small oval "opera windows" on the sides of the folding top. **Left:** In 1926, Ford sold nearly 350,000 Model T Runabouts. **Below:** This 1926 Model T advertisement is aimed at women and touts the car's low $290 starting price.

T he Model T's replacement, the 1928 Model A, still made good use of open body styles. The Touring and Roadster were the price leaders in the series. In 1929, a stylish Cabriolet joined the line, but at a stiff price premium over the roadster. These body styles returned the next year, and in June 1930, a sporty DeLuxe Phaeton debuted. Sharing nothing with the touring or Standard Phaeton, this $645 model was a two-door four-passenger car that saw low production runs in 1930 and again in '31. A late addition to the Model A family was the 1931 Convertible Sedan. It was a four-passenger car with a folding top that tracked up and down on fixed side rails that ran over the side windows. The all-new 1932 Fords reprised most of these styles, but no two-door phaetons.

Top left: In 1928, Model A roadsters could be had with or without a rumble seat for the same $480. **Above:** The cabriolet with its fixed windshield and roll-up door windows brought style to the 1929 Model A line. But it came at a hefty price of $670; nearly 50 percent more than the cheapest $450 roadster. **Left:** Ford sold only 4864 of these 1931 Model A convertible sedans in the United States.

Left: The 1932 Ford roadster was available in standard and DeLuxe form, each with a choice of four-cylinder or V-8 power. This model became the basis for countless hot rods and remains sought after to this day. **Bottom left:** By 1932, Americans overwhelmingly preferred closed cars. One concession to the times was the cabriolet, a true convertible with roll-up windows. In V-8 form as shown here, it was priced at $610. Nearly 6000 were sold in the U.S. **Below:** Cloth and leather interiors were available, each in brown.

Roadsters were on their way out by 1936, but Ford still offered one. It would be gone after 1937. Other open body styles were losing favor with buyers as well, but Ford tried to counter the slide with several changes to the available open models in the second half of the Thirties. For '36 Ford introduced a Club Cabriolet that did away with a rumble seat and moved the second-seat passengers inside and under the folding roof. During the year, the convertible sedan added a new trunkback model that boasted Ford's first concealed spare tire—it stored on the trunk floor. The phaeton was retired after 1938. A curious move came in 1939 when the Club Cabriolet was dropped, but the Convertible Coupe with rumble seat was still listed.

Above: With 14,068 built, the 1936 Ford DeLuxe two-passenger cabriolet was its most popular ragtop. With the rumble seat open, it could seat four. **Right:** The '38 DeLuxe rumble-seat convertible listed for $770, but, in the midst of a severe recession, only 4702 copies were sold. This one, assembled in California, is painted in Desert Sand, a color offered only for the West Coast. **Far right:** The company contended that the '38 Ford's control layout made for "easy driving."

Left: Ford offered two convertibles in 1939, a DeLuxe four-door sedan and a DeLuxe rumble seat coupe. The latter (shown) made good use of the year's sleek new styling. **Bottom left:** The dashboard was neatly trimmed and woodgrained. **Below:** Fords of this era could be equipped with a two-speed rear axle made by Columbia. It offered a high gear for more relaxed—and economical—highway cruising.

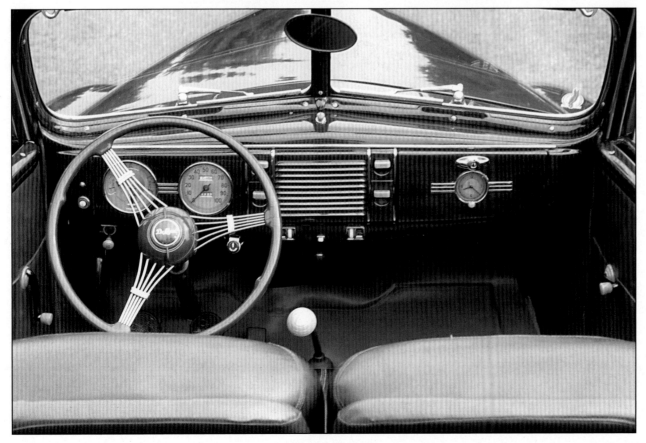

Left: The 1940 Ford convertible was only offered as a dressy DeLuxe model. The rumble seat found on the '39 model was ditched in favor of seating for four inside under the hydraulically operated roof. **Above:** All '40 convertibles had the 85-horsepower version of Ford's flathead V-8.

For the 1940 models, Ford dropped both of the convertible bodies that were offered in 1939. The only open car Ford cataloged in '40 was the new convertible club coupe. It was very similar in concept to 1937's Club Cabriolet with seating for four in the main interior compartment. The hydraulically operated convertible top was big news though. The following season, Ford introduced a line of larger, newly designed cars. The only convertible was in the new top-shelf Super DeLuxe line. Ford had successfully recast the once-price-leader open-air car to one of the most expensive body variations in the line. This basic design would continue on when production restarted after World War II. A second convertible hit Ford showrooms after the war, but cynics may say it was little more than a promotional scheme. The 1946-48 Sportsman was based on the standard convertible body, but with much of the outer sheetmetal replaced with real wood. Sportsman production came to less than 3500 units.

Above left: The '42s wore new front sheetmetal with a flattened grille. Other changes included doors that completely flared over the running boards and rubber stone shields on the rear fenders. The convertible top was revised to allow for rear quarter windows—the change greatly reduced the size of the blind spots with the top up. **Left:** The wood-bodied Sportsman convertible saw its greatest sales success in 1947 with 2250 sold. It listed for $2282, by far the most expensive Ford of the year. This one wears many period accessories including a grille guard, fog lights, fender skirts, and spotlights.

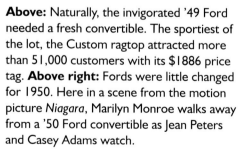

Above: Naturally, the invigorated '49 Ford needed a fresh convertible. The sportiest of the lot, the Custom ragtop attracted more than 51,000 customers with its $1886 price tag. **Above right:** Fords were little changed for 1950. Here in a scene from the motion picture *Niagara*, Marilyn Monroe walks away from a '50 Ford convertible as Jean Peters and Casey Adams watch.

It was a make-it-or-break-it time for Ford Motor Company when the 1949 models were introduced on June 18, 1948. More than 28 million people were reported to have visited Ford showrooms in the three days following the model's debut, and better than 100,000 of the new models were ordered during the first day. Not since the Model A replaced the Model T back in December 1927 had any new Ford created such a stir. The convertible continued to be the showboat of the line, and it was only available in snazzy Custom trim. Ford redesigned again for 1952, and for the first time the convertible was called Sunliner. The following year was the company's 50th anniversary. To help celebrate, the Indianapolis Motor Speedway named Ford's top-line convertible the official pace car for the running of that year's famed 500-mile race. Ford sold more than 2000 pace-car replicas, and the car was popular enough with buyers that some dealers resorted to creating replicas of the replicas.

SUGGESTED RETAIL PRICE LIST

★

1950
EFFECTIVE DECEMBER 13, 1949

Ford

PASSENGER UNITS

COMPILED AND SUPPLIED BY
FORD DEALERS ADVERTISING FUND
WASHINGTON DISTRICT

1950 PASSENGER UNITS		
Deluxe Models	**Six**	**V-8**
Business Coupe	$1,429	$1,515
Tudor	1,520	1,594
Fordor	1,568	1,641
Custom Deluxe Models	**Six**	**V-8**
Tudor	$1,630	$1,709
Fordor	1,677	1,756
Club Coupe	1,630	1,714
Convertible Coupe		2,071
Station Wagon	2,158	2,237

Including Lubrication Policy

OPTIONAL EQUIPMENT
(INSTALLED)

Bumper Guard—Front	$20.85
Bumper Guard—Rear	22.40
Cigarette Lighter—Illuminated	3.95
Clock, Electric (Deluxe Models)	16.20
Directional Signals	19.15
Exhaust Deflector	1.45
Front Fender Side Guard	7.45
Gas Tank Lock Cap	2.25
Heater—Magic Air	57.95
Heater—Recirculating	37.90
Jack, Hydraulic	9.95
Light—Back-Up (Single $7.25) Pair	11.05
Light—Glove Compartment	2.30
Light—Luggage Compartment	1.95
Light—Map	2.55

Lights—Fog	16.00
Light—Spot	19.45
Light—Under Hood	2.25
Light—Utility	1.95
Mirror—Door Top	2.25
Mirror—Glare Proof (Inside)	4.90
Mirror—Outside	3.85
Mirror—Vanity	1.15
Overdrive	96.90
Radio (6-tube)	78.50
Radio (8-tube)	92.30
Radio—Rear Seat Speaker	7.45
Rear Fender Shields	18.00
Rear Window Wiper	15.10
Rocker Panel Trim	12.00
Seat Covers—Composite	23.85
Seat Covers—All Fibre	28.85
Seat Covers—Nylon-Rayon	47.85
Seat Covers—Plastic	48.85
Steering Wheel (Deluxe)	16.65
Sun Visor—Outside—Painted	28.15
Tires—6.00-16 4-ply (WSW)	16.50
Tires—6.70-15 4-ply (BSW) Deluxe Models	12.85
Tires—6.70-15 4-ply (WSW) Deluxe Models	28.40
Tires—6.70-15 4-ply (WSW)	16.50
Tires—7.10-15 6-ply (WSW)	27.90
Undercoating	25.00
Wheel Rings (Deluxe Models) Set of 5	10.80
Windshield Washer	8.95
Window Shades—Exterior (Tudor-Fordor)	15.50
Window Shades—Exterior (Coupe)	8.00
Winterfront	3.95

Above and above right: The Washington District Ford Dealers Advertising Fund compiled this handy suggested price list for the 1950 models. Also listed are the installed prices for optional equipment. **Below:** The Ford Rotunda in Dearborn opened in 1936 and was closed during World War II. It reopened in June 1953 as part of Ford's 50th anniversary festivities. The tourist attraction showcased Ford products and hosted more than 18,000,000 visitors during its run. Fire destroyed the Rotunda in November 1962. **Right:** Henry II's brother, William Clay Ford, drove a Sunliner pace car during the 1953 Indy 500. A replica is shown.

Above: Ford offered striking color combinations in 1955, such as the Tropical Rose and Snowshoe White on this Sunliner. As before, the convertible was only available in Ford's top-of-the-line series, for 1955 named Fairlane.
Right: Color-coordinated interiors helped Sunliner maintain Fifties-fashionable looks.

For 1955, Ford's Sunliner returned with new styling atop the basic design that dated from 1952. America's favorite convertible, with almost 50,000 made for '55, came equipped with a pleated two-tone all-vinyl interior. This sporty looking cabin featured seat centers and backs with horizontal pleats, a motif repeated in the door and side panels. In years past many convertible interiors were only available in a single color, but by 1955 buyers could choose from several fashionable two-tone combinations including red and white, green and white, light blue and blue, yellow and black, and rose and white. A cautious, but pleasing, styling update kept the 1956 Sunliner looking fresh.

Below: Workers prepare to install the body on a 1956 Sunliner. **Right:** The 1956 Sunliner differed little from the '55s. Stylewise the most noticeable changes were a swap of round parking lights for elongated versions, thicker "checkmark" side trim, and a grille that traded the previous year's small squares for a grid of larger rectangles. **Bottom right:** Ford touted "Lifeguard Design" safety features in '56. These included optional vinyl-coated foam padding on the dash and the deep-dish steering wheel.

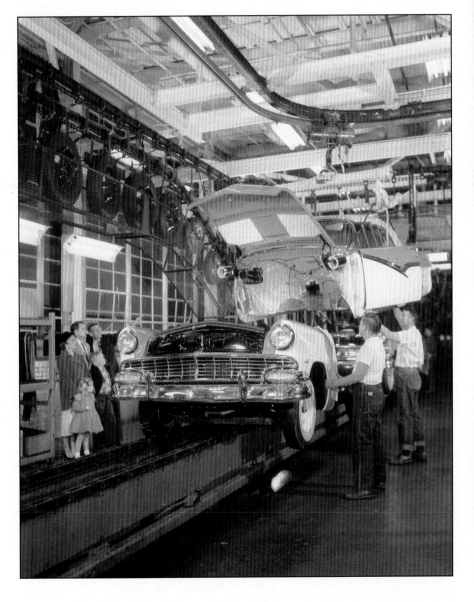

Above and right: There was a lot more involved in the creation of the '57 Skyliner than figuring out how to make the metal top withdraw into and emerge from the rear of the car. Though similar to other Fairlane 500s, Skyliners used a revised frame and specific rear sheetmetal with a rear-hinged deck. **Below:** Like other 1958 Fords, the Skyliner wore Thunderbird-inspired styling cues.

When Ford redesigned its standard models for 1957, the Sunliner rag-top was joined by a second convertible. This one, the Skyliner, had a retractable steel roof. In an era of flamboyant styling and "gee-whiz" engineering features, Ford may have put the "topper" on the period when it introduced the Skyliner. Though it may have looked simple from the outside, the retractable top's mechanism was fiendishly complex with seven purpose-built electric motors, screw-type locks, screw jacks that moved the decklid and the roof, and 610 feet of electric wire. Of course, the top made the Skyliner a "dream car" for the masses. Even then-President Eisenhower found the Skyliner a sensation of the first order, so much so that "Ike" ordered an early example for himself. The Skyliner retractables hardtops were updated along with the other full-size Fords for 1958 and '59. But the novelty wore off, and the retractable Skyliner lasted only three years.

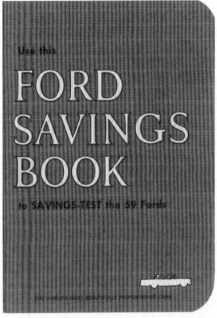

FORD SAVINGS BOOK

Use this

to SAVINGS-TEST the 59 Fords

THE WORLD'S MOST BEAUTIFULLY PROPORTIONED CARS

Now, pick your accessories—add up your savings

CHECK ITEM	ACCESSORY	FORD COST	CHEV COST	YOU SAVE	PLYM COST	YOU SAVE
☐	Automatic Drive No. 1	$189.60	$199.10	$ 9.50	$189.10	$ (.50)
☐	Automatic Drive No. 2	230.80	242.10	11.30	226.90	(3.90)
☐	Overdrive	108.40	107.80	(.60)	107.70	(.70)
☐	Power Steering	75.30	75.35	.05	76.60	1.30
☐	Power Brakes	43.20	43.05	(.15)	42.60	(.60)
☐	Power Seat	63.80	102.25	38.45	48.25	(15.55)
☐	Power Windows	102.10	102.25	.15	102.30	.20
☐	Radio (push-button)	59.50	84.00	24.50	73.00	13.50
☐	Radio (Signal-Seek)	82.80	129.00	30.20	N.A.	
☐	Heater (fresh air)	74.50	90.25	5.75	74.40	(.10)
☐	Heater (recirculating)	48.10	61.90	3.80	N.A.	
☐	Air Conditioner	403.60	468.10(2)	64.50	445.60(3)	42.00
☐	Electric Clock	14.60	19.75	4.15		(4)
☐	Tinted Glass	37.90	43.05	5.15	42.60	4.70
☐	Backup Lights	9.50	13.35	3.85	10.70	1.20
☐	Safety Belts	20.60	29.80	9.20		
☐	Windshield Washer	13.70	12.35	(1.35)	11.80	(1.90)
☐	Tires (8.00 x 14), Black	—	35.85(5)	—	—	

Your total savings on accessories: $ ___ OVER CHEV or $ ___ OVER PLYM

NOTE: (1) Figures in parentheses indicate competitive prices below Ford's; (2) Requires $3.00 x 14 tires—also on 2-door hardtop require tinted glass. Both items included with SelectAire Conditioner at no extra cost; (3) Require tinted glass; (4) Available only as part of Accessory Group costing $29.95.

Above left and left: Squarer styling was ordained for the '59 Fords. Skyliners started the year with Fairlane 500 badges, but a few months later Ford released a sort of "super 500": the Galaxie. At that time, the retractable—and its fabric-topped cousin the Sunliner—were badged as Galaxies. **Above:** Ford released this pocket-size brochure in 1959. Designed to look like a bank savings account book, it detailed how much buyers could save themselves by choosing a new Ford over a Chevy or Plymouth.

As the Sixties dawned, Ford once again offered a single full-size convertible, the Sunliner. As it had been since mid-1959, the Sunliner was part of the premium Galaxie series, but it is interesting to note that Ford didn't install Galaxie badges on the convertibles, only Sunliner scripts. The convertibles closely followed each year's styling changes, and for '62 the Sunliner found itself promoted to the new top Galaxie 500 series. Midyear Ford added a version of the Sunliner in the new Galaxie 500/XL line that also included a two-door hardtop. The XL designated a new bucket seat and center console interior.

This page: The Sunliner looked great in 1960's new big-Ford clothes. Again part of the Galaxie group, Sunliner drew 44,762 sales, slightly down from its 1959 showing.

IS THERE A DRIVER IN THE HOUSE?

Then try this one! When you step in and step down—it moves! No lag. No drag. Just flashing Thunderbird 390 power that's straight from the world's foremost maker of V-8's. Bored with meagre motoring? Want blazing Thunderbird grace and grit? Then let your Ford Dealer open the door to the car that's beautifully built to take care of itself...and everything else on the road!

FORD V-8

Above left: Performance was becoming a more important selling point. This 1961 ad touts Sunliner's available 390-cubic-inch V-8. **Above:** Ford offered $\frac{1}{25}$-scale plastic "promotional" model cars as early as 1949. In 1962, many different models were sent to prospective buyers. This 8-inch-long Sunliner is shown with its original "mailer" box. **Left:** The emblem behind the front wheel announces that this '62 Sunliner packs one of Ford's hottest V-8s.

Above: Ragtop Galaxie 500 convertibles returned for '63 in bucket-seat XL (shown) and bench-seat regular models. **Above right:** For the 1964 model run, Galaxie 500/XLs, including this beachcombing convertible, came with unique spinner wheel covers and an emblem near the rear end of the side trim. A basic bench-seat model was still offered as well.

Ford decided to delete the Sunliner name from the full-size convertibles after '62, but the 1963 drop-tops remained available in bench-seat Galaxie 500 and bucket-seat Galaxie 500/XL forms. The offerings remained the same for the facelifted '64s and the all-new '65s. In '63 Ford added a convertible version of its compact Falcon; the little ragtop was available through 1965. The sporty Falcon-based Mustang hit the market during 1964, and its convertible version sold surprisingly well. In 1966, Ford introduced a third full-size convertible, the Galaxie 500 7-Litre. This model was identified by special wheel covers, unique ornamentation, and a standard 428-cubic-inch engine. Also in 1966, Ford added a drop-top variant of the restyled intermediate Fairlane. Convertible shoppers favored smaller cars as the Sixties wore on, and dramatically lower full-size convertible sales were one result.

Above left: The sportiest big '65 Ford was the Galaxie 500/XL convertible; 9849 were built. The two-door hardtop version was much more popular with 157,284 sold. **Left:** By far the best-selling full-size '66 Ford drop top was the base Galaxie 500. Prices started at $2934. **Above:** As in '66, any 1967 Fairlane GT with automatic transmission, including this convertible, was badged "GT/A." Fairlane ragtops were also offered in base 500 and nicer 500/XL trim.

Right: All big Fords wore new lower-body sheetmetal for 1968. The sporty XL (shown) listed for $3214 and sold 6066 copies. A Galaxie 500 version cost only $106 less, but sold nearly twice as many units. **Below:** This '69 XL has the optional GT package. It was available on any XL hardtop or convertible with a 390- or 429-cubic-inch engine.

By 1968 the new-car market was fragmenting. Through the end of the Fifties, things were much more straightforward. A company like Ford staked out its price range and then garnered most, if not all, its sales from one basic car line. By the late Sixties, Ford had five different car lines in dealer showrooms, and three of them—Mustang, Fairlane/Torino, and Galaxie 500—boasted at least one ragtop. Still, even with the additional choices, Ford's convertible sales were falling quickly. By the early 1970s, Ford began cutting convertible models: the Torino after '71, the full-size LTD after '72, and the Mustang at the end of the 1973 season. With that, Ford was out of the convertible business and 70 years of open Ford cars came to an end; at least until a new Mustang convertible appeared ten years later.

Top and above: For 1970, Ford's only intermediate convertibles were muscular Torino GTs. Just 3939 were built; the tally for the similar '71 model was 1613. **Above right and right:** If you wanted a full-size Ford convertible in 1971, the only choice was a LTD. Though long-time competitor Chevrolet cataloged a big convertible through 1975, Ford threw in the towel after '72.

CHAPTER THREE

Stylish Cruisers

It was a simple idea really: just a closed car without the usual fixed center roof pillar. But greatness often comes from simplicity, and the American hardtop must be considered one of the most significant design developments in automotive history. The idea went back at least to 1915 when Chalmers introduced a body with removable door posts. Not surprisingly the look was quickly copied, but the idea didn't really catch on until General Motors introduced three volume production hardtops—for Oldsmobile, Buick, and Cadillac—in 1949. Chevrolet boasted a hardtop, the Bel Air, by 1950, but Ford could only respond with a flashy two-door sedan, the '50 Crestliner. Then in 1951 Ford introduced the company's first true hardtop, the Victoria. As the body style gained popularity, Ford extended it to four-doors and then to the other car lines the company introduced in the Sixties including Falcon, Fairlane, and Mustang. Despite its widespread popularity, the hardtop disappeared during the Seventies.

Right: Ford's jazzy 1955 Fairlane Crown Victoria was an attempt to combine hardtop looks with the rigidity of a standard pillared sedan. The "Crown Vic" used a wide wrapover "tiara" band to cover the roof posts.

Above: Perhaps the most vivid of the 1950 Crestliner's three color schemes was the Sportsman's Green and black shown here. **Top right:** The Crestliner returned for '51 with larger areas devoted to contrast paint. **Right and far right:** Ford's first true pillarless hardtop was the 1951 Victoria. It went on sale in late January, but still outsold Chevrolet's Bel Air by nearly 7000 units.

The emergence of GM's hardtops in 1949 left car shoppers suddenly smitten with striking two-door cars, and Ford had to have something to offer. The result was the 1950 Crestliner two-door sedan. The Crestliner was offered in three two-tone color combinations, with a sweeping piece of stainless steel side trim separating the two colors. In addition, the exterior wore several visual cues including a basketweave-pattern vinyl top, fender skirts, and specific wheel covers. In January 1951, Crestliner gave way to Ford's first pillarless hardtop, the Victoria. When Ford introduced the redesigned 1952 models, the Victoria hardtop was part of the mix from the beginning.

This page: The Victoria hardtop returned for 1952, now clothed in Ford's new styling. Along with the Sunliner convertible and the Country Squire wagon, Victoria was part of Ford's new top-shelf Crestline series.

This page: Ford tried to give the public something it couldn't get anywhere else with the 1954 Skyliner Victoria. The big draw here was the green-tinted Plexiglas roof insert inspired by Ford's XL-500 show car from 1953. It was a good idea, but in practice the combination of the plastic roof and a sunny day made for perspiring passengers. Aside from the half-plastic top, minor identifying trim, and a price tag $109 higher, it was virtually identical to a standard Victoria.

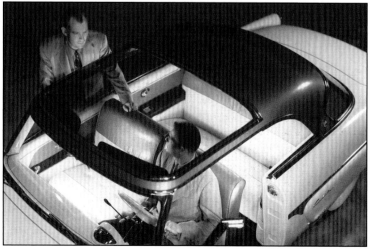

In the mid-Fifties Ford's hardtop Victoria remained in the top-shelf series. In 1953 and '54 this meant Crestline. An interesting variant appeared in 1954, Crestline Skyliner Victoria. Typical of its age, the Skyliner bore an idea lifted straight from a futuristic show car, a transparent plastic roof section. The production car wasn't particularly radical, it was just the ordinary Victoria pillarless hardtop with a green-tinted Plexiglas insert in the roof over the front seat area. Ford painted a happy picture for its new creation, but the green-tinted top made for a slightly weird interior ambience, and Skyliners were notoriously warm inside on a sunny day, this in spite of a snap-in sunshade.

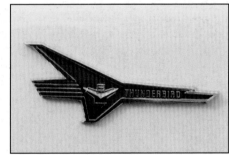

Top left: For only $70, the buyer of a 1955 Fairlane Crown Victoria could add a Plexiglas roof panel in front of the "tiara" trim piece. **Top:** Ford added a pillarless four-door to the line for 1956. The new Town Victoria hardtop sedan found 32,111 buyers. **Left:** The Crown Victoria was still offered with the plastic roof insert for 1956. This example wears many period accessories. **Above:** This small badge announced a Thunderbird V-8 was nested under the hood of a '56 Ford.

Above: In its second season, the airy Town Victoria four door came in Fairlane or Fairlane 500 trim, with a $47 price difference between them. The top seller by more than 5-to-1 was the $2404 Fairlane 500, seen here. **Right:** All '58 Fords, including this Fairlane 500 Club Victoria, wore busier styling. In this recession year, Victoria sales volume slipped by more than 100,000.

For 1957, Ford used two different wheelbases for its "standard" models, but hardtops were only built on the longer span. Club Victoria two-door and Town Victoria four-door hardtops were sold in Fairlane or dressy Fairlane 500 trim. The offerings were the same in 1958, but when the '59s went on sale, the only the Fairlane 500 hardtops appeared. A few months later, a new top-shelf Galaxie series debuted. The new line also included two- and four-door Victoria hardtops, but the Galaxies used a different Thunderbird-inspired roofline. Ford had a new look for 1960 and the only hardtops were Galaxies, a sporty two-door Starliner, and a Town Victoria sedan.

Above: When the 1959 Fords were introduced, the lone hardtops were in the Fairlane 500 series. This year, the hardtop roofline was changed, with the most obvious differences being more upright rear pillars and a larger wraparound rear window. **Left:** Ford only offered full-size hardtops in the Galaxie line for 1960. This Town Victoria four door priced from $2675.

Right: The Galaxie Town Victoria was the only four-door hardtop from Ford in 1961. **Below:** The racy Starliner made its final appearance for '61. **Bottom left:** In '62 all Galaxie 500 two-door hardtops used this boxy roofline. **Bottom right:** Galaxie 500 interiors featured a bench seat up front, along with plenty of bright-metal trim.

Ford styling returned to a more traditional look for 1961. Once again, full-size hardtops were only found in the dressy Galaxie series. The Town Victoria four door was back, as was the racy Starliner with its stylish roof. But a third hardtop appeared this year as well, a Club Victoria that was essentially a two door with the Town Victoria's roof. The look wasn't very dramatic, but the sales were: 75,437 Club Victorias versus 29,669 Starliners. For '62, the full-size hardtop selection was reduced again to two choices; the Starliner was discontinued. The situation changed during the 1963 run when a racier two-door "Sports Hardtop" roofline was introduced to help make Galaxies more competitive "stock-car" racers. The "boxtop" might have been the sales champion, but it wasn't slick enough to claim glory on the nation's big oval superspeedways. As things worked out, the Sports Hardtop not only helped make the '63 Fords a racing legend, the new roof even won the sales race against the boxier Thunderbird-inspired hardtops that were sold alongside.

Right: When the 1963 model run started, the Galaxie 500 and 500/XL (shown) two-door hardtops used this angular Thunderbird-inspired roof that's often referred to as the "boxtop." Mid-year, a second roofline for two-doors, the "Sports Hardtop" was added. It was an inch lower, and miles sleeker.

Another way Ford-built bodies are better built—new longer life electrical systems

Bulbs last twice as long. Taillights, stop lights, turn signals on Ford-built cars keep burning bright.

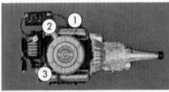

Under the hood: new life. Includes: 1. triple-strength ignition cables; 2. longer-life batteries, self-cleaning spark plugs; 3. extended life distributor points.

Because of the increased electrical demands on today's cars, all 1963 Ford-built cars are engineered to give you longer electrical life. For example, wiring is stronger, distributor points last longer. Even the light bulbs last far longer. And the quality of Ford-built bodies shines through in scores of other ways, too . . . like the solid-riding quiet of the "rigidized" body, the careful fit of the double-panel doors. See for yourself why Ford-built cars last longer, need less care, keep their value better.

Longer life everywhere! New Vinyls have 20% thicker face and 40% heavier backing. Fabrics have all-nylon face. Nylon-rayon carpet is luxurious enough to have in your home.

FORD • MERCURY • THUNDERBIRD • LINCOLN CONTINENTAL

MOTOR COMPANY

FOR 60 YEARS THE SYMBOL OF DEPENDABLE PRODUCTS

Right: The 1964 Galaxie 500 and 500/XL (shown) two-door hardtops used the slippery roofline that debuted during '63. **Below:** Galaxie 500/XLs were fitted with new "thin-shell" front bucket seats for '64. **Below right:** The Fairlane intermediate added a two-door hardtop for 1963.

In the mid-Sixties, Ford hardtops continued to play their role as style leaders. The body style started to transfer to the company's compact and intermediate lines by 1963 when pillarless Falcon and Fairlane models were released. Falcon hardtops would only be offered through '65, but the body style became a fixture on Ford intermediates into the Seventies. In the full-size arena, the sleek Sports Hardtop roofline carried over intact to the '64 Galaxie 500 and 500/XL two-doors, and the four-door hardtops now wore a racier roof inspired by the two-door's lid. Ford redesigned for '65 and the pillarless Galaxies took on new challengers.

"Ford rides quieter than Rolls-Royce." "Oh come now, old boy!"
Lots of people find it hard to believe. But it's a fact—in tests by a leading
acoustical firm, a 1965 Ford LTD with a 289-cu.-in. V-8 and Cruise-O-Matic
rode quieter than a Rolls-Royce. This quiet does not mean
Ford is a Rolls-Royce. But it does mean Ford is strong,
solidly built, designed to give you luxury, comfort and
convenience. Underneath that trim, functional body,
it's all muscle. If you doubt Ford is everything
we say it is, take a test drive and listen...listen hard!

FORD

Top: The 1965 Galaxie 500/XL two-door was popular enough to find 157,284 buyers. **Top right:** Ford added Galaxie 500 LTD two- and four-door hardtops to top the range in 1965. This '65 LTD ad claims Ford's latest rode quieter than that year's Rolls-Royce Silver Cloud III. **Above:** Buyers quickly took to Ford's push into the luxury league, snapping up 101,096 of the '66-model LTDs. **Right:** Ford's Fairlane was redesigned for 1966. The '67s were little changed, but Mario Andretti wheeled a racing version of this '67 500/XL hardtop to victory in that year's Daytona 500.

By 1968, Ford returned to the practice of offering two different rooflines for full-size two-door hardtops. The sporty XLs had what Ford called a fastback. This roofline made for an undeniably dramatic-looking vehicle. The LTD had a more formal-appearing notchback. Interestingly, Ford offered both of these rooflines in the mainstream Galaxie 500 series. Four-door hardtops used a restyled roofline that looked similar to the notchback roof on LTD and some Galaxie two-doors. Then for 1969 Ford had a complete restyle. LTD coupes once again had a notchback profile, but the XL's fastback was replaced with a new tunnel-back design that was dubbed SportsRoof by Ford. Again, Galaxie 500s came either way.

Above: Ford's most popular full-size hardtop for 1968 was this Galaxie 500 two-door with the LTD's notchback roofline. Dealers moved 84,332 copies. A four-door version with a similar profile was also available. **Left:** The Galaxie 500 was also available with the racier roof from Ford's sporty XL. At $2881 to start, it was priced $35 less than the notchback.

Above: Ford called its tunnelback replacement for the fastback roof "Sportsroof" and made it available on the Galaxie 500 and XL. This example wears the optional GT package.
Left: While the luxury LTD was on the upswing for 1970, the sporty XL was down, and nearly out. The two-car series, which included this SportsRoof coupe and the sole big-Ford convertible, suffered a precipitous drop in demand. After the season, the XL—part of the line since mid-1962—was dropped.

Above: Starting at $4097, the LTD Brougham hardtop coupe was Ford's most expensive full-size two-door in 1971. **Top right:** Ford issued this catalog to show company stockholders the 1973 product lineup. Note the LTD two-door hardtop front and center. **Right:** The Gran Torino-based Elite was Ford's answer to the incredibly popular Chevy Monte Carlo. A 1975 model is shown. **Far right:** By time the luxury compact Granada arrived on the scene for '75, opera windows had replaced the hardtop as a style priority.

The pillarless hardtop was the style leader of the Fifties and Sixties, but by the Seventies it was starting to disappear from American cars. Possibly the declining popularity of the pillarless body styles was predicted by the fading away of the convertible in this same era. Another possible culprit was the most prevalent of the many Seventies styling clichés, the "opera" window. Once those small rear-quarter windows appeared on the 1971 Cadillac Eldorado, they were quickly copied by almost every automaker in an attempt to add a touch of class. At first, opera windows were adapted to existing hardtop bodies, but as the decade progressed, the in-demand touch was designed in from the start.

Above and top right: Full-size Fords used pillarless bodies for the last time in 1974, and two-doors used this new roofline starting in '75. GM introduced smaller full-size cars for 1977, but Ford touted the "road-hugging weight" of its '77s like this LTD Landau coupe. **Right:** A carefully placed rib turned this '78 Granada Ghia's opera windows into "twindows."

CHAPTER FOUR

Small Packages

For the first 56 years of its history, Ford sold only one size of car in the U.S. By the late Fifties, the standard Ford was a fairly large car, and smaller compact cars sales were becoming too big a part of the market for Ford to ignore. Ford responded with an economical compact car of its own for 1960, the Falcon. Falcon was a hit from the start, and Ford introduced more small cars as the Sixties progressed. Although Americans have been reluctant to embrace small cars wholeheartedly, every time gas prices fluctuate dramatically, the importance of economical cars becomes apparent. Ford has long built small cars in Europe and, over the years, has occasionally imported these to supplement its domestically built compacts. In recent times, Ford has turned more frequently to its foreign divisions for small cars or assistance in engineering "world cars" that can be sold in all markets—including America. The latest examples of this philosophy—the 2011 Fiesta and 2012 Focus—will be key to Ford's continued prosperity.

Right: Falcon was a hit from the minute it debuted as a 1960 model. Not surprisingly, Falcon received only minor styling changes for its second year. Still, sales rose to an impressive 497,166. The big news for '61 was the addition of a larger version of the Falcon six: 170 cubic inches versus 144 cid for the standard engine. The 1961 Falcon Tudor sedan cost $1914.

Ford entered the blossoming compact car market in 1960 and hit a home run. Falcon rang up 436,000 sales to trump Chevrolet's rear-engined Corvair and Chrysler's odd-looking Valiant, competitors that also debuted for 1960. The Falcon was just 70.3 inches wide and weighed in at between 2300 and 2500 pounds—nearly a foot narrower and more than 1000 pounds lighter than the average full-sized Ford. An all-new 144-cid inline six was initially the sole engine. It delivered 90 horsepower and fuel economy in the 25-30 mpg range. Falcon was available in two-door and four-door sedan, wagon, and "Ranchero" pickup versions. Convertibles and hardtops joined the line later. Robert McNamara, Ford's vice president of North American vehicle operations, envisioned Falcon as economical transportation for the masses and a reasonable profitmaker for Ford, but sportier and more luxurious versions soon joined the base models.

Left and below left: Falcon's simple styling and engineering resulted in a reliable, inexpensive car. The Fordor sedan listed for $1975 in 1960. **Bottom left:** The sporty Falcon Futura debuted in spring of '61 with a plusher interior featuring front bucket seats and center console. **Below:** Futura returned in '62 with minor exterior trim changes. This car is an early model. Later '62 Futuras had a more angular roofline.

Above: A convertible joined the Falcon Futura range in '63. This 1964 convertible started at $2481. The Falcon-based Mustang was introduced in April '64, and it soon stole sales from the sportier Falcons. Falcon sales declined to 318,961 in spite of new sheetmetal for '64. **Left:** The most expensive '65 Falcon wagon was the $2665 Squire identified by its woodgrain trim.

Ford's Cortina: our lowest priced total performance car.

Left: The 1966 Falcon Futura Sports Coupe had a bucket-seat interior and top-line trim. Total Falcon sales dropped below 183,000. **Below left:** The 1968 Falcon Futura sedan gained side-marker lights to meet new Federal requirements. **Above:** In the Sixties, Ford imported the Cortina compact from its British operations. The 1966 prices ranged from $1765 to $3420 for the racy Lotus-Cortina with a twincam four. **Below:** Ford needed an alternative to sales-stealing imports and found it in the compact 1970 Maverick, introduced on April 17, 1969.

Left: The 1971 Pinto two-door sedan started at just $1919. A 76-hp four was the base engine. **Above:** Pinto added a station wagon model in mid '72. By 1973, the wagon was Pinto's most popular body style. **Below:** Thanks to the energy crisis, sales of the thrifty Pinto reached 544,209 in 1974. Two overhead-cam four-cylinder engines were offered: a 122-cid unit with 80 hp and a 140-cid version with 82 hp.

The all-new Falcon for '66 was based on a shortened midsized Fairlane and returned to its roots as a basic, affordable compact. Even more affordable and compact was the Maverick introduced for the 1970 model year. Nineteen seventy would be the last year for Falcon as Maverick took its place as Ford's compact car. Mavericks didn't have cutting-edge engineering, but with attractive styling and a starting price of $1995, more than half a million were sold during the first year. The even smaller Pinto subcompact came out in 1971. Challenging the imports and Chevrolet's new Vega, Pinto offered a low price and fuel economy that was better than anything else in the Ford lineup. Pinto outsold the trouble-prone Vega by moving almost 350,000 cars its first year. Though Pinto served Ford well during the energy crises of the Seventies, it will be remembered for a rash of highly publicized (and, in some cases, fatal) fires following rear-end collisions that revealed the vulnerable fuel tank and filler neck design of the 1971-76 sedans.

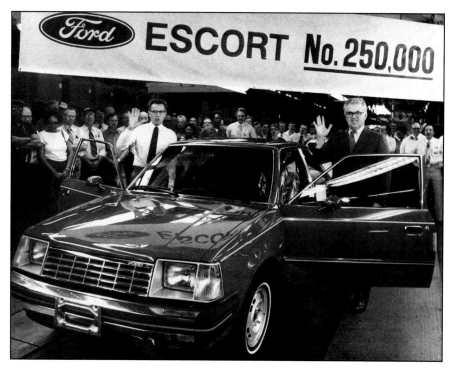

The industry was moving to front-wheel drive for economy cars in the Seventies, and Fiesta was Ford's new front driver. Although a European project, Fiesta was designed with the American market in mind. The first Fiestas were exported to the U.S. for the 1978 model year and had a 1.6-liter four-cylinder engine developing 66 hp. In America, Fiesta and Pinto were replaced in 1981 by the "world car" Escort that was built in five countries—including the U.S. Escort was a modern front-drive subcompact with four-wheel independent suspension, and soon became the second best selling car in the U.S. with 320,727 delivered the first year. Ford, on a front-drive roll, introduced Tempo for 1984. Tempo was slightly larger than Escort and sold 402,000 its first year. Not as successful was the tiny Festiva built for Ford by Kia of Korea and introduced in 1993. Festiva was a slow seller in spite of its low $6914 base price. In 1998, the Escort line was expanded with the sporty ZX2 coupe that had more power and a firmer suspension.

Top left: Prices for the '78 Fiesta started at $3680 for the bare-bones base model, though it could be dressed up with the Ghia or Sport packages. **Top:** This final-year 1980 Pinto wagon has the $606 Cruising package that included graphics and port-hole windows. Portholes were popular on customized vans during the Seventies. **Above:** Sales vice president Phillip Benton (right) waves as he stands alongside the 250,000th Escort to roll off the line at Wayne, Michigan, on May 13, 1981. From day one, Escort sold better than its Pinto predecessor.

Top left: An all-new Escort had more aerody-namic styling for 1991. The base wagon cost $9680. **Top right:** Tempos sold well, and in '93 sales had a surprise spurt to 238,000. After 1994, Tempo was replaced by Contour, which never matched Tempo's showroom success. **Left:** Festiva was only 140.5 inches long—two and a half feet shorter than the Escort. That small size contributed to an impressive EPA fuel-economy estimate of 42 mpg highway. **Above:** The 1999 Escort ZX2 coupe shared its platform with the less exciting Escort sedan and wagon. However, it sported Contour's dual-overhead-cam, 130-hp engine—20 hp more than the standard Escort.

Left: The 2000 Focus was available as a two-door hatchback, four-door sedan, and four-door wagon. **Above:** While overseas markets got a redesigned Focus replacement for 2005, the U.S. made do with a freshening of the 2000-design Focus. Standard horsepower rose from 110 to 136. **Below:** Focus got a more serious updating for 2008 with fresh styling. Only a two-door coupe and four-door sedan were offered. The sole engine was a 140-hp 2.0-liter four cylinder.

Focus debuted in 2000 to replace both Escort and Contour. Focus was a masterpiece of space utilization, offering more passenger and cargo room than the cars it replaced. Initial engines were 2.0-liter fours—110-hp single cam and 130-hp twin cam. The suspension was all-independent and drew rave reviews for ride and handling. Despite a flurry of early recalls, the Focus was an unqualified success, drawing more than 389,000 orders its first year. Focus began to feel dated and was substantially updated for 2008 with fresh styling and new features. For the 2011 model year, Ford reintroduced Americans to the Fiesta nameplate. The new Fiesta weighed just over 2500 pounds. Its light weight contributed to good fuel economy and lively handling. Prices started at $13,320. An all-new Focus was expected to arrive in the States in early 2011 as a 2012 model. Ford said Focus was a true world car with only relatively modest tailoring for the local needs and tastes of American, European, and Asian markets.

Above left: One of the new features of the freshened 2008 Focus was the debut of Ford's Sync. Developed with Microsoft, Sync provided voice control of certain MP3-player and cell-phone functions. **Above:** The 2011 Fiesta came in four-door sedan or four-door hatchback (shown) form. In the U.S., the sole engine was a 119-hp, 1.6-liter four. **Left:** Ford CEO Alan Mullaly previewed the 2012 Focus at the 2010 International Auto Show in Detroit. U.S.-market cars received a clean-sheet 2.0-liter four-cylinder with direct fuel injection and variable valve timing.

CHAPTER FIVE

Ponies & Snakes

Mustang, the original "pony car," was Detroit's greatest single success of the Sixties. Announced six months ahead of model-year 1965, it lifted Ford volume by well over half a million and set an all-time record for inaugural new model sales with 680,099 sold during its long introductory season. The Baby Boomers were starting to drive, and Mustang tapped into the youth market beyond all expectations. When the pony car craze seemed to be over, Mustang reinvented itself as the small, fuel-efficient Mustang II, just in time for the 1973 oil embargo, and sales took off again. The Mustang II was right for its era, but it didn't have the excitement diehard Mustang fans desired. A larger, but still trim, Mustang arrived in 1979. As the Eighties progressed, V-8 power increased and Mustang was back on track. There were further ups and downs, but through it all Mustang enthusiasts remained loyal and Ford rewarded them with rear-drive, V-8-engined cars that remained true to the Mustang tradition.

Right: One of the best movie car chases was in *Bullitt* with Steve McQueen driving a Highland Green Metallic 1968 Mustang (background). In 2001, Ford offered a Bullitt package on the GT coupe (foreground). Production was limited to 6500.

Above: The $2614 Mustang convertible was popular, and 101,945 were sold during the 1965 model year. **Right:** Lee Iacocca is known as the father of the Mustang. Although Iacocca didn't develop the Mustang single-handedly, he sold the concept to Henry Ford II and ensured its production. The Mustang phenomenon was national news, and Iacocca was on the cover of both *Time* and *Newsweek* the same week in April 1964.

The formula for Mustang was simple: a reasonably priced, sporty, personal car based on high-volume Falcon components. Riding a compact 108-inch wheelbase, Mustang pioneered the pony-car concept with its long-hood/short-deck silhouette, bucket-seat interior, and long options list. Prices started at $2372, putting Mustang within reach of a large number of car buyers. Those with deep pockets could personalize the car through a wide array of luxury and performance options. The Base engine was the Falcon's 170-cid 101-hp straight six; optional was a 260-cid V-8 good for 164 ponies. After the first six months of production, Mustangs got a standard 200-cid six with 120 hp and bored-out 289-cid V-8 options with 200-271 hp. Initially, Mustang offered hardtop coupe and convertible body styles, but a fastback coupe (or 2+2) was added midseason. The 2+2 had less backseat room but could be ordered with a fold-down rear seat for increased cargo room. Ford didn't mess with a good thing and made few changes for '66.

Wolfgang used to give harpsichord recitals for a few close friends. Then he bought a Mustang. Things looked livelier for Wolfgang, surrounded by bucket seats, vinyl interior, padded dash, wall-to-wall carpeting (all standard Mustang)...and a big V-8 option that produces some of the most powerful notes this side of Beethoven. What happened? Sudden fame! Fortune! The adulation of millions! Being a Mustanger brought out the wolf in Wolfgang. What could it do for you?

Best year yet to go Ford
MUSTANG!
MUSTANG!
MUSTANG!

Above left: First-year ads claimed Mustang could change your life. Although planned as a youthful car, Mustang ads were pitched to all ages. **Above:** This 1966 Mustang fastback is equipped with the popular GT package that included four-barrel carburetor, stripes, and fog lights. **Left:** Ford staged elaborate publicity shots of the '66 Mustang featuring split lens taillights. But Ford axed those taillights at the last minute to save costs and returned to the original 1965 style.

Right: Carroll Shelby poses with a production Cobra (left) and Cobra race car (right). With the 289-cid Ford V-8, the road car could do 0-60 mph in 5.5 seconds. **Below:** The 1965 Shelby Mustang GT-350 could accelerate 0-60 mph in 6.8 seconds and top 120 mph all-out. The backseat was deleted to save weight.

Left: Starting in 1965, Shelby put 427-cid V-8s in Cobras for blistering acceleration—0-60 in 4.2 seconds. This '67 Cobra 427 S/C has the rare semi-competition equipment. **Below:** By '68, Shelby Mustangs had morphed into more-civilized "grand-touring" machines, here a GT-500. Also, a convertible version was debuted. **Bottom:** Restyled for '69, the GT-500 was powered by a 428-cube V-8 conservatively rated at 335 horses.

When heart trouble forced Carroll Shelby to retire from racing after he won the LeMans 24 Hours in 1959, the one-time Texas chicken rancher turned to building fast road cars. The first were the legendary Shelby-Cobras. Starting with the lightweight Ace roadster from A.C. Cars in England, Carroll replaced its small six-cylinder with a potent Ford V-8. Shelby built about 1000 Cobras from 1962 to '67. Lee Iacocca asked Shelby to modify the Mustang so it could win the Sports Car Club of America's national B-production championship. The resulting GT-350 did just that in 1965-67. Shelby built road versions as well. The GT-350 was a Mustang fastback with a 289 V-8 modified to produce 306 horsepower. In 1967, a GT-500 with a big-block 428-cid V-8 joined the GT-350. The 1969 GT-350 switched to a 351-cid V-8 with 290 hp. As the years went by, Shelbys became more like stock Mustangs. After 3150 of the '69s, plus 636 leftovers sold as 1970 models, Shelby and Iacocca agreed to end the Shelby Mustang program.

Why see a marriage counselor?
Get a Select Shift.

...has a better idea

Above: New for '67 was Select Shift, a three-speed automatic transmission with manual override. **Right:** Drag racers were quick to seize on the potent 428 Cobra Jet V-8 that became an option in '68. Mustang fastbacks were always a threat in the Super Stock class. **Below:** The '67 2+2 got a sweeping new full-fastback roofline.

Ford refined the Mustang for '67. The lower sheetmetal was new, but didn't stray far from the original styling. Inside was a new twin cowl dashboard. Suspension was revised for better ride and handling. A big-block 390-cid, 320-hp V-8 was a new option. In spite of these improvements, sales were down as Mustang faced competition from the new Chevy Camaro/Pontiac Firebird and restyled Plymouth Barracuda, as well the Mustang-based Mercury Cougar. For '68, a 427-cid V-8 was introduced, then replaced midyear by Ford's new 428 Cobra Jet that was conservatively rated at 335 hp. The '69 Mustang was longer, wider, and heavier. A new Mach 1 with firm suspension and standard 250-hp, 351-cid V-8 joined the line at $3139. Two low-production Bosses were also new: a Boss 302 with a 302-cid V-8 and a Boss 429 with a 429 V-8.

Left: The '69 Boss 429 (foreground) was ready-made for the dragstrip, while the Boss 302 (background) was a street version of Ford's Trans-Am racer. **Below:** The 1969 Mach I featured handling suspension, upsized wheels and tires, and a surprisingly posh cockpit.

Above: The 1970 Mach 1 gained optional rear window louvers. Mach 1 production totaled 40,970 units. **Right:** With buyer tastes changing, Mustang convertible sales fell to a low 7673 in 1970. **Below:** The SCCA's Trans-American Championship was launched to take advantage of the popularity of pony cars. Parnelli Jones won five of Ford's six victories in 1970 in a Boss 302.

The restyled 1969 Mustang was mildly facelifted for 1970. Sales dropped below 300,000, but racing was a bright spot as the Boss 302 won the Trans-Am Championship—ending a two-year drought. The big change came in 1971 and "big" was the key word. The new '71 was the largest Mustang ever; eight inches longer overall, six inches wider, and close to 600 pounds heavier than the '65 original. A 370-hp, 429-cid V-8 was the most powerful engine in the lineup, but it only lasted the year. There was only one Boss in '71: a Boss 351 powered by a 330-hp 351 V-8. The Boss was also dropped after '71. Mustang sales dropped below 150,000 as changing tastes sent the pony car market into steep decline. Most changes for '72 and '73 were to meet mounting government regulations, but a major shift was coming.

Right: The Mustang fastback was pitched only 14 degrees from horizontal. It looked racy but played hob with visibility. This 1971 Mach I has flat-face hubcaps. **Below:** Ford added a "Sports Hardtop" in April 1971 with Boss/Mach 1-style hood and grille, body-color bumper and side stripe, plus a "halo" vinyl top. Though it cost a mere $97 more than the regular hardtop, only 500 were sold. **Below right:** This 1972 standard hardtop started at $2729.

As the pony-car market dwindled, the bloated Mustangs of the early Seventies were out of step with what the public wanted. Lee Iacocca knew a smaller, more economical Mustang was needed. A fuel-efficient Pinto-based Mustang II was in the pipeline several years before the oil embargo of 1973. Two months after Mustang II's introduction, America was rocked by its first Energy Crisis and any small car flew off the dealer's lot. The thrifty Mustang II was almost as big a hit as the original. Performance was threatened in the Seventies by tightening emission regulations and a new need for fuel economy. Mustang II emphasized handling and luxury instead. Initially, two engines were offered: a 2.3-liter 4-cylinder and a 2.8-liter V-6. In 1975, a small 302-cid V-8 was added. The notchback coupe returned, the fastback morphed into a hatchback, and the convertible was dropped.

Above: Lee Iacocca was the driving force behind both the 1974 Mustang II (foreground) and the original 1965 Mustang (background). **Left:** The 1974 Mustang II rode on a 96.2-inch wheelbase and was 20 inches shorter, four inches slimmer, and 400-500 pounds lighter than the '73 Mustang. This base four cylinder coupe started at $3031—up $321 from its larger '73 six-cylinder counterpart.

Above left: The 1976 Cobra II was an appearance package for hatchbacks. The option did nothing to make the car go faster. **Above:** Fresh-air fiends applauded the new T-bar roof option for '77 hatchbacks (left). The Cobra II (right) returned for '77 with new color schemes and an available Sport Performance Package that added actual muscle. The option included a 139-hp V-8 engine and sport suspension. **Left:** With standard V-6, the 1977 Mach 1 hatchback could go 0-60 mph in 13-14 seconds and reach 100 with the standard four-speed manual. This was a far cry from the Boss and big-block days but was almost spirited by mid-Seventies standards.

Above left: A trio of '81 Mustangs: a sunroof-equipped hatchback sits above plain-roof and T-top notchbacks. **Above right:** The Mustang convertible returned in 1983. Here an '84 GT-350 20th anniversary model (foreground) poses with a classic '65. **Right:** The '85 Mustang SVO was powered by a 2.3-liter turbocharged four with 205 hp. SVOs had performance suspension, uprated brakes, and unique styling.

Although the Mustang II was the right size for the energy crisis, most thought it was the wrong size for a Mustang. In 1979, a new, bigger Mustang emerged based on the "Fox" platform shared with Ford Fairmont and Mercury Zephyr. The '79 Mustang was built on a 100.4-inch wheelbase and had five inches more rear legroom but, because of lightweight materials, weighed 200 pounds less than a comparable Mustang II. The Fox-based Mustang was a winner, and the platform served Mustang through 2004. As time progressed, advancing technology allowed the return of performance. Mustang's top horsepower rose from 140 in '79 to 235 in '93.

Top left: This 1986 Mustang LX has an optional fuel-injected 5.0-liter (302-cid) V-8 with 200 hp. **Top right:** A new, smoother nose helped lower the '87 GT hatchback's drag coefficient to a worthy 0.38. The 5.0 V-8's horsepower was up to 225. **Left:** For almost $1000 less, this '91 LX with 5.0 V-8 offered all the GT's V-8 muscle without the added flash. Mustang sales dropped below 99,000 in the recession year of '91. **Above:** The 1993 Mustang SVT Cobra hatchback had a 235-hp V-8, good for 0-60 in under six seconds. The Cobra was conceived by Ford's Special Vehicle Team. Starting at $20,000, the Cobra boasted 17-inch wheels, recalibrated chassis, and unique styling touches. Just 4933 were built.

Above: The '94 Mustang V-6 started at $13,365. All Mustangs now had dual airbags and four-wheel disc brakes. **Above right:** The '94 GT V-8 ran 0-60 in 6.1 seconds and the quarter-mile in 14.9 at 93 mph in *Car and Driver* testing. **Right:** The 1995 SVT Cobra R had a 300-hp, 351-cid V-8. Only 250 were built: all white coupes with bulging fiberglass hoods and no weighty backseat or air conditioning. The price was $35,499.

Mustang was mostly new for '94. Receiving its first major redesign since 1979, the new Mustang had fresh styling that borrowed cues from the 1965 original. The Fox platform carried over, but the body was more rigid and suspension was massaged for better ride and handling. The four-cylinder engines were gone, replaced by a base 145-hp V-6. The V-8 was the trusty 5.0 liter now with 215 hp in GTs or 240 in Cobras. After 40 years of service, that overhead-valve 5.0-liter V-8 was replaced in '96 by a 4.6-liter overhead-cam unit. Mustang was revamped for '99 with crisp-edged styling. Once again the body was stiffened and the suspension was improved. The Fox platform continued to serve Mustang well.

Left: The restyled-for-1999 GT convertible started at $24,870. **Below left:** Ford PR staged an "air" shot evoking the climactic scene of the Steve McQueen movie *Bullitt* with a 2001 Bullitt coupe. Bullitts had 265 hp—five more than the GT's V-8. **Below:** The limited-production 2003 Mach 1 recalled Mustang's past with a functional "shaker" hood scoop. Its 4.6-liter V-8 produced 300 hp, 40 more than the Mustang GT.

Above: The Mustang GT accounted for about 30 percent of 2005 Mustang sales. GTs continued the Mustang tradition of most performance for the buck. **Right:** A Shelby GT 500 joined the Mustang lineup in 2007. It was powered by a 500-hp supercharged 5.4-liter V-8 and had performance suspension.

No new Mustang was ever newer than the 2005 model. The '05 was the first Mustang that didn't share its underskin architecture with an existing Ford product. It enjoyed, in the words of chief engineer Hau Thai-Tang, "a purpose-built, muscle-car chassis new from the ground up." The new platform made possible a redesigned suspension tailored to Mustang's cost and performance requirements. Styling once again picked up cues from Mustang's past. A new base 4.0-liter V-6 put out 202 hp, while the carried-over 4.6-liter V-8s had new heads and saw output rise to 300 hp. In 2010, Mustang was revamped with freshened styling and an upgraded interior. Two new all-aluminum, dual-overhead-camshaft powerplants arrived for 2011. The 3.7-liter V-6 put out 305 hp—more power than the V-8 was producing only five years earlier. The 5.0-liter V-8 developed a healthy 412 hp. The world and the American car market keep changing, but for more than 45 years Mustang has remained innovative and perpetuated a loyal following.

Above: Ford commemorated the 40th anniversary of the Steve McQueen movie *Bullitt* with a version of the 2008 GT coupe. The Bullitt package included more power, special exhaust system, and tweaked suspension. **Right:** The 2010 V-6 convertible started at $25,995. **Below:** This 2011 GT coupe has optional Brembo brakes and xenon headlights. GTs gained an all-new 5.0-liter V-8 for '11.

CHAPTER SIX

Dearborn Dandies

Starting on top is one thing, staying there quite another. Ford created an instant classic with the first Thunderbirds, the 1955-57 two-seaters that became some of the most recognized and beloved cars of their time. The replacement that came along in 1958, the four-seat "Squarebird," may not be as memorable, but the bigger car sold spectacularly well and helped define the elements of "personal luxury"—bucket seats, center console, power everything, and sporty-yet-dignified styling. This formula was soon widely imitated. Over time, Thunderbirds became progressively begadgeted and bedazzled because that's what customers seemed to want. The Seventies would put a change to that, with the energy crisis and government-mandated fuel economy standards forcing smaller, more rational T-Birds. Ford retired the Thunderbird after the 1997 model run, but a reprisal in 2002 harkened back the classic two-seat model. As it turned out, the new car wasn't able to rekindle the magic of this legendary nameplate.

Pride inspired the two-seat Thunderbird, but profit was the main motivator behind its four-seat replacement. The so-called "Squarebird" enjoyed a three-year run that culminated in the 1960 model shown.

A personal car of distinction . . .

FORD THUNDERBIRD

Thunderbird's legacy began with a two-seat convertible that was low, sleek, and powerful, yet defied the "sports car" label. Boasting luxury features unknown to its competitors, Ford instead categorized it as a "personal car." The Thunderbird project hatched in February 1953, barely a month after Chevrolet's Corvette debuted at the General Motors Motorama in New York. Ford readied its response quickly and displayed a wooden mockup of its two-seater at the Detroit Auto Show in February 1954. The Thunderbird name wasn't decided on until shortly before the car's Detroit unveiling. Ad agency J. Walter Thompson suggested more than a thousand names, but most were pretty lame: Astro-Flame, Cruisejet, Picturesque, Ty Coon, and Wombat to name a few. The winning name came from Ford stylist Alden R. "Gib" Giberson. His prize: a $250 suit. Sales commenced on October 22, 1954. The announced base price of $2695 wasn't exactly cheap, and the figure soon went to $2944—just $10 more than a Corvette. The first year, 16,155 found buyers.

Above: The cover art on this 1955 brochure helped define what Ford wanted the Thunderbird to be. It wasn't a sports car, but a "personal car of distinction." Style, comfort, convenience, and luxury were important ingredients of the new Thunderbird. Sports car traits like handling and braking weren't as crucial.

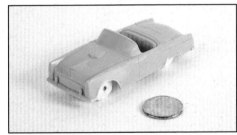

Above left: Thunderbirds, like this 1955 model, were soon status symbols in stylish suburban neighborhoods. **Top:** To help promote the year's new cars, small plastic models of 1955 Fords were included in some boxes of Post Grape-Nuts Flakes cereal. **Above:** The simple, three-inch-long toys, like this Thunderbird, were made by F&F Mold and Die Works of Dayton, Ohio. **Left:** Thunderbird received its first major styling changes for 1957. The fiberglass hardtop was removable.

This page: Nearly 800 pounds heavier, the '58 was a substantially bigger 'Bird. The blocky profile later prompted this Thunderbird generation's "Squarebird" nickname. Unitized construction dictated tall door sills and a beefy transmission tunnel, but the latter was made "functional" with the addition of the industry's first console.

Left: Changes for 1959 were minor. A horizontal-bar grille replaced 1958's honeycomb design, with this theme repeated for the taillight surrounds. **Below:** Styling was little changed for 1960, but sales rose by more than a third to 90,643. New options included a manually cranked sliding sunroof for hardtops.

A quest for higher sales—and profits—prompted a larger four-seat Thunderbird. Though lower in profile than workaday Fords, the new 'Birds were by no means "sporty," since luxury took the center stage. Edgy styling and a host of features proved popular with buyers. Sales and profits took off, cementing Thunderbird's future at Ford. The new 1958 model debuted as a two-door hardtop coupe—the convertible didn't reach dealers until June 1958. Wheelbase was up 11 inches from the two-seat car, and Thunderbird now used unitized construction that did away with a conventional frame. Ford's new FE-Series V-8 engine was featured along with a standard Cruise-O-Matic three-speed automatic transmission. Inside, the new Thunderbird used individual bucket-type seats up front and the industry's first tunnel control console. Both items remain sporty-car features to this day. This second-generation Thunderbird design was used through the 1960 model year. For the three-year run, sales totaled more than 196,000 units, nearly quadruple the two-seat car's sales tally.

Above: Ford continued to stress elegance in Thunderbird advertising. **Right:** Two of the 1961 Thunderbird's most notable styling features were the projectile front end and the chrome-capped sweep from the front bumper to the tip of the fins. **Below:** The new interior featured a more prominent console and a "Swing-Away" steering wheel that eased entry and exit. **Bottom right:** The rear was marked with large round tail-lamps that recalled jet-engine exhausts. As before, the new T-Bird bowed in two body styles, here the $4172 hardtop.

Top: Predictably, the follow-up '62s showed only slight visual changes. The rear fenders now sported three louverlike ornaments, and the grille swapped horizontal bars for small chrome squares. **Bottom:** New for '62, the Sports Roadster was intended to satisfy those yearning for a two-seat Thunderbird. A removable fiberglass tonneau covered the rear seats. A rare 1963 model is shown; only 455 of the '63s were sold.

Now an established—and profitable—member of the Ford family, Thunderbird was given a sleek new "bullet" shape for 1961. Ads called it "Unique in All the World," and in many ways it was. Certainly it was like nothing else in Detroit, though the T-Bird would have direct competition by the time this generation was through. Under the hood, a larger V-8 engine was made standard, though performance still took a distant back-seat to luxury. An optional 390-cubic-inch V-8 with triple two-barrel carbs and 340 horsepower arrived for 1962, along with a pseudo-two-seat model. Both were interesting, but neither proved very popular with buyers.

Top: The all-new 1964 body sported busy side sculpturing, a prominently bulged hood, and a drop-center rear deck with large, rectangular taillight nacelles. **Bottom left:** Changes for 1965 included a chrome "C-spear" on the front fenders. **Below:** Hardtops, like this '66, had a full-width vent under the backlight that helped ventilate the interior.

A busy 1964 for Ford Division was a pivotal year for the Thunderbird, again fully redesigned for a three-year stand. The new fourth generation bowed amidst a flock of sporty Detroiters with bucket seats, floorshift, and, in many cases, a center console—features pioneered by the 1958 "Squarebird." Imitation is the sincerest form of flattery in Detroit, and it was the four-seat Thun-derbird's consistent success that inspired General Motors to field its own personal-luxury cars in the 1962 Pontiac Grand Prix and, more directly, the 1963 Buick Riviera. Ford was aware of both some time before they appeared and planned the 1964 Thunderbird to one-up these and any other upstarts. The resulting '64 was a luxury liner with no gesture to performance.

Left: The 1966 model was the last Thunderbird convertible until 2002. An available tonneau recalled the 1962-63 Sports Roadster, but sportiness wasn't really part of this Thunderbird's appeal. **Bottom left:** Bright trim and a host of knobs adorned the dash. **Below:** The '66 facelift included a toned-down hood scoop, a taller grille, and a slimmer "blade" front bumper.

The fifth-generation Thunderbird arrived for 1967 and was arguably the purest expression of personal luxury yet seen from Ford: larger, heavier, and plusher. Ford had carefully gauged the market and concluded this was the way to go, at least with the way things looked in 1964 when work on the new car began. Though sales belied that conclusion, the '67 established the 'Bird's shape, size, and character for the next decade. Symbolic of the new order was Thunderbird's first sedan, an idea debated for several years by Ford managers. Though vestiges of past designs were present, the new car's appearance was appealing and fresh.

Opposite page top: Thunderbird saw big changes for 1967 including a new four-door Landau model and the return of body-on-frame construction. Rear-hinged "suicide" back doors were used. **Opposite page bottom:** The new design also came as a two-door, here as a base 1969 hardtop. **This page:** The 1970 models broke the Thunderbird's usual three-year design cycle with a heavy facelift of the 1967-69 'Bird. The prominent, vee'd snout was an obvious styling change. In this form, the two- and four-door Thunderbirds carried into 1971 (shown) with little more than a new grille.

Top: Ford shifted sales tactics for 1972, offering just a single hardtop coupe that could be personalized with optional trim and equipment. This one wears the $137 Landau option. **Right:** By 1975, the Thunderbird had received the government's required "5-mph" bumpers front and rear.

Taking the "bigger is better" approach, the sixth-generation Thunderbird was as large as the car would ever get. The 1972 arrived as a single two-door hardtop on a 120.4-inch wheelbase, and it shared many components with the Lincoln Continental Mark IV. The new car sold better than the previous T-Bird in the fast-changing market, this in spite of an unprecedented energy crisis. Even so, necessity was the mother of the radically different seventh-generation Thunderbird that was introduced for 1977. It is easy to dismiss this smaller Thunderbird as a gilded midsize Ford—that's what it was—but it flew out of showrooms like no other T-Bird.

Top left: The new-for-1977 T-Bird was actually a deft reskinning of the five-year-old platform used on Ford's midsize Torino and Elite. The resulting car was 10 inches shorter and 800 pounds lighter. **Top right:** Added brightwork on and around the headlamp doors was the only notable change for 1978. Sales for the year were 352,751—the best tally ever for Thunderbird. **Right:** A more open grille design marked the 1979 models. Removable glass roof panels joined the options list the previous year.

Above: The 1980 Thunderbird, here a Town Landau, was basically an upscale, slightly larger spinoff of Ford's popular Fairmont compact. **Top right:** Ford announced a new direction for the company's styling with the dramatic 1983 Thunderbird. This 30th Anniversary edition was released in 1985. **Right:** The handsome 1989 car was offered in muscular Super Coupe form with a supercharged V-6.

Thunderbird's eight, ninth, tenth, and eleventh generations share little visually and demonstrate how Ford tried to keep the Thunderbird relevant in a quickly changing market. The car entered the Eighties with a much smaller package and angular styling. This basic car was dramatically reskinned for 1983 with smooth aerodynamic lines. The so-called "Aerobird" was heavily facelifted for 1987. Two years later, an all-new T-bird surfaced on a fresh chassis. It lasted through the 1997 model year, then Ford shelved the name. A new two-seat Thunderbird concept was shown at the Detroit Auto Show in early 1999. It went into production for 2002 and was discontinued after the 2005 run. The name was again retired.

This page: Ford trotted out a modern take on the classic two-seat Thunderbird as a concept at the Detroit Auto Show in early 1999. This prototype clearly displays classic T-Bird design cues updated for the new century. A V-8 engine and rear drive were other nods to Thunderbirds past.

CHAPTER SEVEN

Total Performance

Henry Ford built his first racing car in 1901. He drove it in a 10-mile sweepstakes event at Grosse Pointe, Michigan, and won, beating the heavily favored Alexander Winton. It was the only race Henry ever participated in, but it brought him national attention. In 1904, Henry set a world speed record of 91.37 mph, bringing himself, and his young Ford Motor Company, attention in the newspapers. Over the 100-plus years that have passed since Henry last drove a racer, the company he founded has often embraced—and triumphed in—competition on the world's racetracks. Ford used the experience gained to develop and improve the company's image and products. Likewise, Ford has sold numerous cars and trucks with exceptional performance that everyday consumers could use and enjoy on a daily basis. Among large automakers, Ford may have conceived and produced the widest-ranging array of performance machines. Many can be considered among the most successful and memorable of their eras.

Ford's Special Vehicle Team (SVT) was tasked with finding new ways of creating and marketing high-performance vehicles. This 1999 SVT family portrait shows the Contour (front left), F-150 Lightning (rear left), and Mustang Cobra coupe (front right) and convertible.

Right: The "999" and its sibling the "Arrow" were 80-horsepower monsters that first raced during 1902. Daredevil Barney Oldfield, and Henry Ford himself, set speed records in the cars. Oldfield and other drivers barnstormed tracks across the country with the racers and helped cement Ford's early reputation for performance. **Below:** Henry Ford tinkers with his monoblock "flathead" V-8 that entered production in 1932. It was the first mass-produced, low-cost V-8.

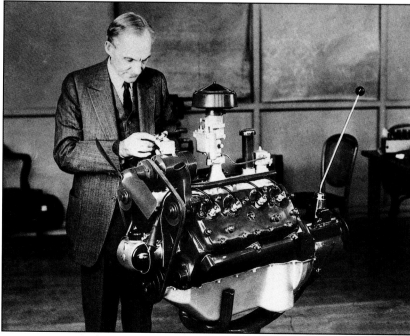

Henry Ford's earliest motor-racing exploits pre-date today's Ford Motor Company, founded in 1903. Henry won a race in 1901, and in 1902 he built a racing car that enthusiasts remember to this day, the "999." Other racers followed. Henry even tried to enter a Model T-based racer in the 1913 Indianapolis 500. Though Henry's greatest sales success came with the 4-cylinder-powered Model T, his low-cost "flathead" V-8 of 1932 introduced this engine type to the mass market. The flathead made its mark in competition by 1933, and the engine quickly became a favorite of the "hot-rod" set. To this day, souped-up flatheads power many hot rods. Ford made a multicar assault on Indianapolis for 1935, but the embarrassment that followed the failed effort sidelined the company's racing efforts for nearly two decades.

Above: Dirt track and speed boat racers were among the first to discover that with a few simple modifications, a Ford V-8 would outperform most everything else its size and weight. Stock car drivers soon found that by stripping the running boards, fenders, and top from a regular V-8 roadster and making a few chassis adjustments they could beat just about anything on the dirt tracks. At the famous Elgin, Illinois, road race in August 1933, stunned onlookers watched as seven stripped Fords took the top seven spots in a highly touted field of Chevrolets, Plymouths, and Dodges. Here, Frank Brisko takes a corner at speed in the #14 Ford V-8 on his way to a fifth-place finish. **Left:** Four front-drive flathead-powered Miller-Fords qualified for the 1935 Indianapolis 500. None finished.

Ford dipped its toe back into the racing pool in 1955, mostly in reaction to the Chevrolets running on the NASCAR circuit. Ford built two '55 Ford sedan racers in Dearborn, Michigan. Charlotte, North Carolina, dealer Schwam Motors painted them purple and went racing. Ford won twice in '55 and 14 times in '56. For 1957, Ford countered Chevy's fuel-injected 283-cube V-8 with a supercharged version of the Thunderbird's 312 V-8. Horsepower was advertised at 300, but some say the blown engine was really making 325 ponies—the hot Chevys were good for 283 horses. The new Fords were nearly unstoppable on the track, but a one-page memo from Henry Ford II changed that. The Automobile Manufacturers' Association (AMA) agreed to a ban on racing and performance activities. On May 17, 1957, the edict came down from the top: Ford was out of racing. That would change.

Top and above: Ford had to build supercharged 312 V-8s—and sell them to the public—to be able to use the engine in NASCAR competition. In addition to the company's "regular" models, Ford offered the 300-horsepower mill in the freshened '57 Thunderbird. The so-called "F-Code" engine added $500 to the 'Bird's price; only 208 were sold. **Right:** Racers preferred the lightest, low-line Custom two-door sedan in '57. Here, one makes a speed run on the beach at Daytona.

Left: The Ford-powered Shelby Cobra first took to the racetrack at Riverside in October 1962. Bill Krause led until a rear hub failed and ended his day. **Below:** Ford tried to sneak the slippery add-on "Starlift" top for Sunliner convertibles past NASCAR for the 1962 season. Ford wanted this roofline for superspeedway racing, but officials nixed the idea after one race. **Bottom right:** Ford had to run the boxy production Galaxie roofline instead. **Bottom left:** The hottest mill in '62 was this 405-horse 406-cube V-8.

Wait till you feel Fairlane's Sunday punch!

FORD

Above: The Fairlane added a 271-horsepower 289 V-8 for 1963. **Top right:** Fred Lorenzen won six races and nearly a quarter-of-a-million dollars behind the wheel of his #28 Holman-Moody prepared '63½ Galaxie on the NASCAR circuit. **Below:** The slippery '63½ Galaxie Sports Hardtop was two inches lower than the equivalent notchback and allowed a great aerodynamic advantage on NASCAR's superspeedways. **Right:** Two Lotus-Ford racers were entered in the 1963 Indianapolis 500. Jim Clark finished second in the green-and-yellow #92.

Ford officially honored the AMA racing ban until June 1962. For 1963, Ford started to get serious about racing. The 1963½ Galaxie 500/XL Sports Hardtop was one of the first obvious statements of the company's renewed interest in competition. The slant-back roofline was clearly aimed at making Ford more competitive on the nation's oval racetracks. The company also took on the big two-and-a-half-mile oval at Indianapolis with two Ford-powered rear-engine Lotus single seaters. Total Performance became a major selling point for 1964, as numerous Ford products and Ford-powered racers took to circuits in North America and Europe.

Top left: Falcons ran the Monte Carlo Rally in '63 and '64. **Top:** "Cobra tonic" for '64 Fairlanes added extra horsepower via dealer-installed Cobra kits. **Above:** Ford unleashed 127 of these 427-powered '64 Fairlane Thunderbolts for drag racing. **Left:** Even Ford's ¹⁄₂₅-scale plastic promotional models trumpeted Total Performance in '64. Here, a Galaxie 500/XL ragtop with its "mailer" box.

Right: In 1965, the full-size Galaxie was still Ford's weapon of choice for stock-car racing. Here, Fred Lorenzen wheels his #28 around the road course at Riverside, California.
Bottom: In his third appearance at the Brickyard, Jim Clark won the 1965 Indy 500 in this Ford-powered Lotus 38.

Total Performance really came together during 1965 and 1966. There were many highlights. A Shelby-prepared Ford GT40 won the 1965 running of the Daytona 24-Hour Race. Jim Clark won the Indy 500 in a Ford-powered Lotus. Ford-powered Shelby Cobra Daytonas won the World Manufacturers Championship for sports cars. Disputes over the Hemi engine meant Dodge and Plymouth teams were parked during the 1965 NASCAR season. Ford took full advantage of the situation, as Galaxies won 48 of 55 events in NASCAR's top series. In 1966, GT40 Mark IIs won at Daytona, Sebring, and LeMans. Ford looked unstoppable.

Left: Ford GT40 Mark II #2, driven by McLaren and Amon, on its way to winning the 24 Hours of LeMans in '66. Above: Henry Ford II enjoys LeMans victory. Below left: Topping the '66 Galaxie 500 line was the new 7-Litre, named for the metric size its 428-cube V-8. Below: Ford ran off a small batch of 427 Fairlanes in '66.

Left: A Torino GT ragtop paced the 1968 Indy 500. **Below left:** Ford's ultimate '69 race engine, the new "semi-hemi" Boss 429. **Below:** David Pearson won NASCAR titles in '68 and '69 driving Torinos. Here he sits in a new '69 "droop snoot" Torino Talladega. **Bottom:** New for '69, the "budget-muscle" Torino Cobra traded on Pearson's on-track success.

By 1968, the muscle car era was nearing its pinnacle. Ford maintained performance as a company priority, on and off the track. Ford repeated the 1966 LeMans triumph three more times, with the final win coming in 1969. Fairlane replaced the Galaxie in stock-car racing for 1967, and for '68 the torch was passed to the new Fairlane-based Torino. Street performance increased its swagger as "tough" appearance packages and special models came into vogue. On the engine front, big-block V-8s remained important. In 1969, Ford tried to gain an upper hand on Chrysler's mighty Hemi with the Boss 429. Looking back, street muscle peaked in 1970, and it faded into the rear view mirror surprisingly quickly.

Left: Torino was redesigned for 1970, but the sleek new body proved aerodynamically disappointing on the nation's super-speedways. The hallowed Cobra name still graced the main performance model. **Below:** Under this Cobra's shaker scoop sits the new-for-'70 429 Cobra Jet engine with 370 horsepower. **Below left:** Ford's *1970 Performance Buyer's Digest* cataloged the company's performance cars, parts, and engines. **Bottom:** The redesigned 1972 Torino put on pounds and inches. The hot model was this GT Sport fastback.

Right: Ford's answer to Chevy's 454 SS pickup was the 1993 F-150 Lightning with its 250-horsepower 351 V-8. It listed for $21,655 and only came in two-wheel-drive form. **Below:** The high-performance Taurus SHO bowed for 1989 with a 220-horsepower "Super-High Output" 3.0-liter V-6 engine built by Yamaha in Japan. Shown is a 1993 SHO. An automatic transmission was a new option for '93; previously, a 5-speed manual was the only transmission available in the SHO.

Ford never completely left the street performance game during the Seventies, but the available products were nothing like they had been in 1970. By the late Seventies, performance was defined more by appearance packages and tape stripes than actual hardware. The reborn Mustang GT of 1982 may have been the first sign that horsepower was ready to make a comeback. It did, but brute, straight-line performance was not always the goal. V-8 engines remained part of the performance formula, but six- and even four-cylinder powerplants had roles to play as well. Midsize performance returned with the debut of the Taurus SHO for 1989.

Left: Ford's Special Vehicle Team (SVT), which was also responsible for recent Mustang Cobras and the F-150 Lightning, conjured up this Contour SVT. A modified 2.5-liter V-6 put out 195 horses. **Bottom left:** SVT unleashed the race-ready Mustang Cobra R in 2000. Packing a 385-horse 5.4 V-8, it could do 0-60 in under five seconds. **Below:** The second-generation F-150 Lightning debuted for 1999 and was significantly upgraded for 2003. An '03 Lightning went better than 147 mph at Ford's proving grounds that August.

Above: Zippy, sport-compact "tuner" cars skyrocketed in popularity around the turn of the century. Ford's entry in this booming market was the Focus SVT. **Below:** Having lost the rights to the legendary GT40 name, Ford's 2005 reinvention of its 1966 LeMans racer was known simply as the GT. Though strikingly similar to the classic GT40 Mark II, the new car was significantly larger. A supercharged 5.4-liter V-8 put out 500 horsepower. Prices started north of $130,000.

In the first decade of the new century, Ford's performance story continued to evolve—in some ways the company borrowed from past glory but with an eye towards the future. In 2002, the company introduced a SVT-tuned version of its front-drive Focus compact and at the same time showed a GT40 concept car that paid obvious homage to Ford's LeMans-winning racer of the Sixties. The Focus SVT was discontinued by the time limited-production Ford GTs hit dealers in 2005. All during this time, Mustangs became progressively hotter, and an all-new retro-styled version arrived in 2005. In the later part of the decade, gas prices became quite unstable and it was becoming clear that modern performance cars would have to do with less fuel. Ford's response? EcoBoost, a combination of various technologies including turbocharging and direct fuel injection.

Left: Stock-car racers haven't been very closely related to street-driven cars for decades. Matt Kenseth won the 2009 Daytona 500 in this purpose-built Ford Fusion. It shared little beyond its name with Ford's midsize family sedan.
Below: Ford dropped the Taurus SHO following the 1999 model run. It was reprised for 2010 when Ford's big sedan was redesigned. The new SHO gets a 3.5-liter V-6 with Ford's new "EcoBoost" technology that includes a pair of turbochargers and high-pressure gasoline direct injection. The result is 365 horsepower—102 more ponies than the naturally aspirated 3.5 V-6 in lesser Taurus models. There is little penalty in fuel economy despite the added power. All SHOs get a 6-speed automatic transmission and all-wheel drive. Prices start at $37,995.

CHAPTER EIGHT

Serve & Protect

Historians tend to portray the early days of law enforcement as officers walking their beat while swinging a truncheon. But police have always used vehicles—in one form or another. Horses and carriages were common in earlier days, as were bicycles and motorcycles. As America moved into the 20th century, motorized vehicles began to appear in police fleets. Ford products have served many police departments over the last 100-plus years. Model Ts helped put America on wheels, and likely did the same for countless police agencies. The debut of the "flathead" V-8 in 1932 was welcome news for police—and criminals liked it as well. Legend has it that in April 1934, serial robber Clyde Barrow sent a letter to Henry Ford praising the Ford V-8. Ford offered the first car tailored specifically for police use in 1950; it was a package of special components available for Ford sedans. In recent years, the Ford Crown Victoria—now known as the Police Interceptor—has dominated police-car sales in the U.S.

A dedicated group of enthusiasts collects and restores old police cruisers. This 1951 Ford sedan wears the colors of the Illinois State police.

Right: There were all kinds of uses for the trucks made from the heavy-duty Model T chassis. This one from the late Teens served and protected for an unidentified police department. **Below:** Like other early V-8 models, the 1937 Fords were used by many agencies. Note the red lights and siren, early examples of such equipment.

One of the initial police uses for trucks and large touring cars was to transport special squads of officers to trouble spots—hence the term squad cars. Early on, auto manufacturers realized the importance of this market and catered to it with special vehicles. This peaked during the Prohibition era, when some were fitted with machine-gun ports, armor plating, and bulletproof glass. When the Depression set in, police departments were hit just as hard as the public. Fleets were curtailed, and the vehicles purchased reflected that austerity. Ford's introduction of the potent flathead V-8 in the inexpensive 1932 Model 18 was a boon to police agencies working with slashed budgets. This period also saw changes in the traditional police network, with many state highway patrols being organized during the 1930s. Meanwhile, radios (some being merely one-way) gained strong acceptance, as did markings that identified police vehicles.

Left and above: This 1941 DeLuxe Tudor was pressed into service with the Connecticut State Police. It cost $772 without the added police equipment.
Below: Just outside of Chicago, the Lincolnwood Police Department had a single motorcycle and two cruisers for patrol: a 1941 Super DeLuxe Tudor (left) and a similar 1942 model.

Left: These sparkling new 1946 Ford Tudor sedans are lined up for review. Equipment includes two-way radios and an advanced-model siren/red light on the roofs. **Above:** San Diego law-breakers faced a tight squeeze into the back seat of this 1948 coupe sedan. **Below:** Aside from the few pieces of police-specific equipment, San Diego officers worked in a basically unmodified interior.

After World War II, the typical police department fleet was filled with well-used patrol cars. As they had been before the war, frisky V-8 Fords were popular choices for postwar police duty. Of course, Ford V-8s were also popular with the speed-obsessed hot rodders many police officers were chasing down. A more modern, completely redesigned Ford debuted for 1949. The new Ford wasn't a slouch. *Popular Science* set the 0-60-mph time at 16 seconds; a car running the 4.10:1 overdrive rear end could do it in less than 15.5 seconds. Cornering ability wasn't great, but the new chassis design didn't wander on high-speed straightaways like the '48 did. By 1950, Ford released a special police package for sedans; this meant a specially equipped car especially suited to the demands of police work was available from the factory for the first time. Chevrolet didn't respond to this development until its own V-8 engine came on line for 1955.

Top left: The Michigan State police added new 1949 Fords to its fleet. Note the front- and rear-facing roof-mounted red lights. **Above:** In 1952, the Houston Police Department drove Customline two-door sedans. **Left:** Zanesville, Ohio's plain white '53 Mainline was assigned to traffic control duty. **Below:** The Highway Patrol Division of the Texas Department of Public Safety used Ford's 1954 Interceptor police car. The vehicle had a specially developed 160-horsepower V-8 engine capable of pushing the car to more than 100 mph.

1956 FORD

Available with the new "Interceptor" Y-8 Engine of 215 h.p.
and Lifeguard Design features for greater safety

Preferred by

Law Enforcement Agencies

everywhere

POLICE

Left: The police market was important enough that Ford released specific police-car catalogs, including this one on the 1956 models. The hot new 215-horsepower "Interceptor" engine was mentioned on the cover. **Below:** In 1957, Ford squad cars could be fitted with the "Thunderbird Special" engine, rated at 245 horsepower.

As the Fifties progressed, Ford offered more and more special equipment for police use. Ford's 1956 police catalog details specific items including Special Police and Interceptor V-8 engines, upgraded generators, special brake linings, and a specially designed heavy-duty radiator. Other heavy-duty items included clutch, springs, shocks, and floor-mats. Special "24-hour duty" seats were installed front and rear with heavy-gage springs and specific padding. Ford's standard upholstery and trim could be replaced with washable brown vinyl at extra cost. Police agencies could choose from Customline and Mainline Tudor and Fordor sedans, a six-passenger two-door Ranch Wagon, or six- and eight-passenger Country Sedans.

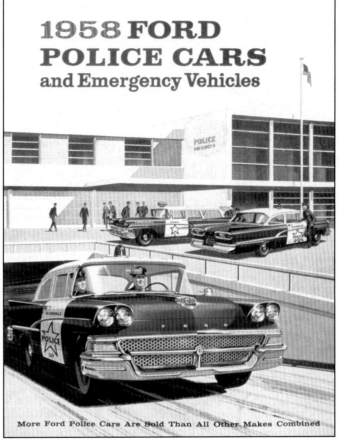

1958 FORD POLICE CARS and Emergency Vehicles

More Ford Police Cars Are Sold Than All Other Makes Combined

Top left: Customs were popular police cars in 1958. This Texas State Patrol two-door sedan is fitted with spotlights, Motorola radio, and the 300-horsepower Thunderbird Special "Interceptor" 352 V-8, one member of Ford's newest engine family. **Above:** Ford's 1958 police car catalog bragged that Ford sold more police cars than all other makes combined. **Left:** Ford police cars were usually based on low-line Custom 300s rather than Fairlanes like the Town Sedan shown here.

Left and below: Big Fords were still much favored by "John Law," be it in real life—as evidenced by this restored Columbus, Georgia, patrol car—or on television, where Sheriff Taylor and Deputy Fife served the good folks of Mayberry. **Bottom:** The *1965 Ford Police Cars* catalog detailed the year's law enforcement offerings.

In Ford's "Total performance" era, police departments weren't left to fend for themselves. According to the *1965 Ford Police Cars* catalog, police could choose from the widest variety of models ever, 41 different car and wagon styles. Each model had its own name tied to the engine fitted. Among the full-size models, the big dog was the Police Interceptor with its 330-horsepower 390 V-8. Then came Police Cruiser with a 300-horse 390, Police Guardian with a 352 V-8 rated at 250 horsepower, and Police Sentinel with the small-block 289 V-8 good for 200 ponies. The Police Deputy was fitted with a 150-hp "Police Special" six. Fairlane squads ranged from the Police Defender with a 225-horse 289 V-8 to the Police Sentry with a 120-hp six. In both series, two- and four-door models were listed.

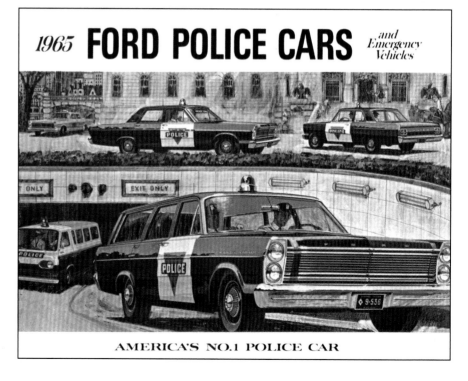

1965 FORD POLICE CARS *and Emergency Vehicles*

AMERICA'S NO. 1 POLICE CAR

Above: With "civilian" Fairlanes competing in the muscle-car wars, police-package Fairlanes were available with significantly more horsepower under the hood. In 1966, a 335-horse 390 was the top option. **Right:** Full-size Ford police cars were available with four different engines in 1971. At the top of the heap was the Police Interceptor with a 370-horse 429-cube V-8.

By the late Seventies, police departments were facing the same realities as the car-buying public. With higher fuel prices, smaller and less powerful cars were becoming the norm. Though Ford previously listed Fairlane and Torino police packages, in 1978 Ford offered an even smaller cruiser in the form of the new Fairmont compact. A downsized big car arrived in 1979, and though updated several times, the basic car was still built more than 30 years later. Ford entered new territory in 1982 when it supplied the California Highway Patrol a fleet of 5.0-liter V-8-powered Mustang coupes for high-speed pursuit work. Top speed was nearly 130 mph. Though a police version of the front-drive Taurus sedan was offered, Ford's mainstay in the police market continued to be the big rear-drive sedan.

Top left: The 1978 Fairmont compact gained a police package midyear. It only came in a four-door version. **Top:** Ford's big-car offering for 1982 was the LTD, but it didn't compare well with the police cars offered by Chrysler and GM. **Above middle:** The Fairmont-based LTD became Ford's midsize police offering by 1984. **Left:** Following California's lead, Florida used 1986 5.0-liter Mustangs for the patrol-pursuit duties of its Highway Patrol. **Above:** Redesigned for 1992, the full-size Crown Victoria was Ford's traditional police car offering.

Left: The police package versions of the front-drive Taurus and traditional rear-drive Crown Victoria for 1995. **Below left:** Ford's Crown Victoria received a fresh look for 1998. By the time this 2003 model was introduced, Ford used the Police Interceptor name for its law-enforcement mainstay. The basic car remained in production through 2011. **Below:** A Taurus-based Police Interceptor replaced the Crown Victoria unit. It offered a standard 3.5-liter V-6 with front-wheel drive, or the 365-horsepower EcoBoost V-6 from the Taurus SHO paired with all-wheel drive.

CHAPTER NINE

Working Class

Ford eased gently into the truck market it would one day dominate. The first Ford truck was a 1905 delivery vehicle. It lasted only one year. Ford was content to let outside suppliers build a variety truck bodies for early Ford chassis. Ford even built the heavy-duty TT to accommodate them. Not until 1925 did Ford offer the factory pickup bed on the Model T. Because the Model T was a rugged car to begin with, it made a solid truck. The Model T Pickup proved a success, and Ford finally got serious about the truck business. Ford introduced its F-Series pickups in 1948. Initially called the F-1 in ½-ton form, the designation became F-100 in 1953 and this nomenclature continues to designate F-Series pickups to this day. Ford vans and sport utilities became popular in the Seventies. In the Nineties, when SUVs ruled the American market, Ford's Explorer was the top seller. With rising fuel prices, trucks and SUVs may be less important, but Americans will always need trucks and Ford continue to build them.

Ford didn't let the 50th anniversary of its F-Series pickups pass unnoticed. Numerous promotions depicted the 1948 version (background) with a new 1998 model: in this case, an F-150 regular cab with luxury Lariat trim.

Left and above: Station wagon forerunners such as this Depot Hack—so named because it ferried passengers to and from a train depot—were bodied by outside suppliers. This one rides a 1914 Model T chassis. **Below:** A one-ton truck chassis listed for $600 in 1918. This example hosts a canopy-covered passenger compartment for weather protection, along with a stake-bed body.

In the early years, Ford was content to let others build truck and commercial bodies on bare Model T chassis. In 1917, Ford introduced the one-ton Model TT, but it came with only a cab. The TT had a strong frame and worm-gear differential, along with solid-rubber rear tires—all aimed at providing a much higher payload capacity than the light-duty Model T chassis. The first all-Ford-built pickup was the 1924 TT. It was quickly followed by a Model T pickup in 1925. This was a roadster with its rear deck replaced by a pickup bed. The Model T was replaced by the Model A in 1928, and the roadster pickup was joined by a closed cab model. A sedan delivery also joined the line. Ford built its first station wagon in 1929. Early station wagons were commercial vehicles and were rarely bought for family use. Ford introduced a V-8 in 1932 for cars only, not in trucks—odd, since it was a natural for heavy-duty haulers. Truck buyers clamored for the new engine, and it was phased into trucks during late 1932. In '33, Ford cars became lower and more streamlined. Trucks needed more ground clearance than cars, and Ford truck styling and engineering started to go their separate ways.

Above left: Ford's first real pickup was introduced for 1925. The Model T Runabout with Pick-Up Body cost $281. Ford built 33,795 pickups in '25. **Above right:** The 1929 Sedan Delivery was basically a standard Model A Tudor sedan with filled-in rear windows, no back seat, and a rear cargo door. **Right:** Two Santa Monica Canyon lifeguards pose with their '33 Ford V-8 pickup in this 1948 photo. Although a four-cylinder was offered, most '33 pickups were powered by the 75-hp V-8.

Above: Unlike the car-like Sedan Delivery, this 1936 Panel Delivery was truck-based, so it carried truck styling. **Right:** Ford trucks got new styling for 1938 with a more spacious cab and larger cargo box. The pickup cost $590. **Below:** To ease shipping to all theatres of WWII, the Ford-built version of the Willys Jeep was packed in crates. Ford built 270,000 of the Army's General Purpose vehicles during the war.

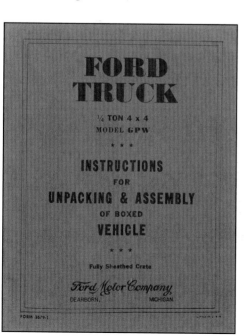

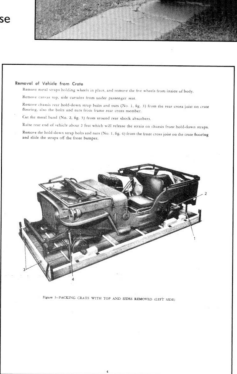

By 1935, Ford was building only V-8s; the slow-selling fours were dropped. Despite the success of the V-8, Ford was sometimes criticized for not offering an "economy" engine. So in 1937 the company responded by adding a radically downsized V-8. The small V-8 produced 60 horsepower versus 85 for the standard V-8. A larger 95-hp V-8 was added in 1939. That same year, Ford made the switch from outdated mechanical brakes to hydraulic. The smaller V-8 was just too small and was replaced by a six in 1941. Also in '41, Ford started production of military Jeeps. Production of civilian vehicles stopped on February 10, 1942. Civilian truck production resumed in 1945 with a warmed-over '42 design to get assembly lines moving as quickly as possible. In 1948, a new era began with the release of a redesigned line of trucks Ford dubbed the "F-Series." In 1951, cabs were restyled. The following year, Ford switched its six-cylinder engine from side to overhead valves.

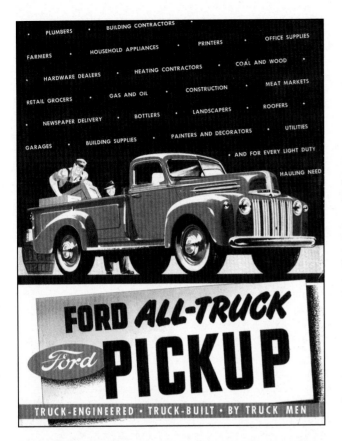

FORD *ALL-TRUCK* PICKUP

TRUCK-ENGINEERED · TRUCK-BUILT · BY TRUCK MEN

Top left: Ford built 78,088 ½-ton pickups for 1946 and could have sold more in the postwar seller's market, but steel and other materials were still in short supply. **Top right:** Along with the fresh styling given 1948 Ford trucks came new model designations; this ½-ton was labeled F-1. **Above:** The 1949 F-1 Panel Truck had a generous 160.3 cubic feet of cargo room. **Right:** This 1952 F-1 pickup is powered by a 101-hp overhead-valve six.

Left: The 1954 F-100's standard ohv six was enlarged to 223 cid, and horsepower increased to 115. **Above:** A new wrap-around windshield and revised grille were the foremost changes for the 1956 F-100 pickup. **Bottom left:** The restyled 1957 F-Series was powered by a 139-hp six or 171-hp V-8. **Bottom right:** The base 1957 Ranchero started at $2098. Top engine option was a 292-cid, 212-hp V-8, which wasn't offered in other trucks.

Left: Like most manufacturers, Ford switched to quad headlights for 1958, applying them to both cars and trucks. For the F-Series, that meant a restyled grille—which they had been getting every year anyway. **Below:** The factory 4WD available on ½-ton F-100s and ¾-ton F-250s included a two-speed transfer case and was capable of climbing 60 percent grades. An F-250 is shown.

Nineteen fifty-four brought the end of Ford's famous flathead V-8, which was replaced by an overhead-valve V-8. The new 130-hp V-8 displaced the same 239 cubic inches as the outgoing side-valve but produced nearly 15 percent more horsepower. A restyled 1957 F-Series was available with a choice of two pickup beds: the traditional Flareside, with a narrow bed and attached rear fenders; and a new Styleside, with a full-width bed and straight-through fenders. Also introduced in '57 was the new car/truck hybrid called the Ranchero. Based on a two-door station wagon platform, it combined Ford's car styling with the utility of a pickup by replacing the wagon's covered cargo area with an open bed. In 1959, for the first time in Ford history, a light-duty truck buyer could buy a factory-built four-wheel drive. Previously, Ford trucks were converted to 4WD by outside companies such as Marmon-Herrington.

Top left: The long-running *Ford Almanac* provided farmers and cityfolk useful information and interesting facts while promoting Ford vehicles. **Top right:** The 1961 Econoline utilized a trim 90-inch-wheelbase chassis and tucked the engine and transmission up inside the cab beneath a sound-deadening cover. Despite having just an 85-hp, 144-cid Falcon six, the lightweight Econolines were useful haulers and easy on gas. **Left:** In 1960, Ranchero adopted the compact Falcon's unibody design and sales increased 50 percent over the full-sized '59s. Ranchero greeted 1962 with a fresh face that included a new grille and pointed fenders, but little else was changed. **Opposite page, top left:** This F-100 is equipped with new-for-'65 Twin-I-Beam front suspension and 352-cid V-8. **Opposite page, top right:** The 1966 Bronco pickup-style Sport Utility started at $2480. Out of 23,776 Broncos sold that year, 6930 were pickups. **Opposite page, bottom:** Ford's F-100 and F-250 (shown) had all-new styling and roomier cabs for 1967.

Ford's successful compact, the Falcon, spawned a new smaller, lighter Ranchero in 1960. The popular Ranchero was followed in 1961 by another Falcon derivative, the Econoline series. Also known as the E-Series, the line included a cargo van, a passenger van, and a pickup truck. The van was literally a box on wheels, the pickup being a box with the top rear quarter removed. The F-Series was redesigned in 1961 with new cabs and revamped interiors. Ford's famous Twin-I-Beam front suspension debuted in 1965 on 2WD F-150s and F-250s giving them a softer ride and better handling characteristics. The Bronco sport utility vehicle was launched in '66. Aimed squarely at the Jeep CJ and International Scout, the 4WD Bronco was available in three body styles: Roadster with no top or doors; Wagon with a removable metal top; and Sport Utility with a removable metal top and a very short pickup bed. All had a folding windshield for truly open-air driving. A 170-cid six was standard, but a 289-cid V-8 was added later as an option. Also in 1966, Ranchero grew in size because the Falcon on which it was based moved up to the midsized Fairlane platform. While Ranchero grew, Econoline, the other Falcon-based vehicle, remained relatively unchanged. In 1969, Econoline was redesigned for the first time since its 1961 introduction. It emerged much larger. Econoline lost its pickup derivative but gained its first V-8 option.

Above: Econolines received a new grille, and a 240-cid six was standard in all models for '71. **Right:** Ford's domestically built light trucks for 1973 included (clockwise from left) the Bronco, F-100, and Ranchero. **Below:** The Econoline-based 1977 Cruising Van was Ford's way to cash in on the custom van craze of the mid 1970s.

Ford responded to import trucks in 1972 with a captive import from Mazda of Japan. The Ford Courier was a compact pickup with a four-cylinder engine. Also in '72, Ranchero was updated. In '73, it was the F-Series turn for a redesign. The next year F-Series got its first extended cab, which allowed buyers to carry extra passengers or more cargo inside the cab. It was Econoline's time to shine for 1975, sporting its first redesign since 1969. But what would turn out to be an even bigger event—though it was hardly that at the time—was the introduction of a "heavy ½-ton" F-Series called the F-150. Bronco underwent its first major redesign in '78. The new version was substantially larger and better equipped.

Above left: This 1978 F-100 Custom has the Free Wheeling Package that included stripes and special trim. **Above right:** The new for '78 Bronco was derived from F-Series trucks. A 351-cid V-8 was standard, with a 400 cid available. **Left:** Courier was redesigned for '77. Front turn signals moved from the bumper to the grille for '78. Styling was relatively unchanged through '81 when this Courier was built.

The slow-selling Mazda-built Courier was replaced by the Ford-built Ranger for 1983 and quickly became the most popular compact pickup in the land. Ranger provided a base for the compact '84 Bronco II sport-utility vehicle. The full-sized two-door Bronco SUV continued until 1997 when it was replaced by an the bigger still four-door Expedition. The F-100 was discontinued for 1984, but the slightly beefier F-150 absorbed F-100 buyers—as evidenced by the fact it would soon become the nation's best-selling full-sized pickup, and soon after that the best-selling vehicle of any type. The Ford Explorer replaced Bronco II for '91 and quickly became the best-selling SUV in the U.S. The 1997 F-Series was a completely redesigned full-sized truck that featured the most radical changes yet seen from one generation of Ford pickups to the next. Initially, only certain models of the new F-Series were offered, so some 1996-style trucks continued to be sold along side them. The F-250 HD and F-350 weren't redesigned until the 1999 model year. Among the F-Series' many accolades in '97 was the coveted Truck of the Year from *Motor Trend* magazine. In 1998, Ford Motor Company celebrated the 50th anniversary of the F-Series brand. At the smaller end of the truck scale, Ranger received a longer cab and larger standard engine, along with an electric-powered model. Ford closed the century with booming truck sales.

Top left: Ford's new Ranger compact pickup looked much like a scaled-down F-150. Prices started at $7068 for a standard short bed like this one. **Top right:** The 1984 Bronco II was 19 inches shorter and 800 pounds lighter than its big Bronco brother. All models came with four-wheel drive and a 2.8-liter V-6. **Above:** F-Series trucks, including this F-350 crew cab, got an aerodynamic restyle for 1987. Optional was a 6.9-liter diesel V-8 built by International Harvester. Dual rear wheels for this model were made available beginning in 1985.

Left: Shown here in top-of-the-line Eddie Bauer trim, the new 1991 Explorer redefined the sport-utility segment and quickly became a sales leader. **Below left:** The F-Series was redesigned for 1997. A top-line Lariat regular cab is shown. **Below right:** The 1997 Ranger was available in sporty Splash trim with a standard Flareside bed. **Bottom:** The redesigned for 1999 F-350 was available as a SuperCab with dual rear-hinged doors. Super Duties (F-250 Heavy Duty and F-350) were identified by grilles incorporating vertical "nostrils" at each edge.

Ford began the 21st century by releasing a new super-sized sport-utility vehicle bigger than anything else on the market—or that had ever been on the market. Called the Excursion, it rode on the Super Duty truck chassis that also hosted Ford's F-250 HD pickups. Balancing the huge Excursion SUV was the compact Escape introduced in 2001. Also in 2001, the F-150 gained a crew cab version dubbed SuperCrew. It marked the first time a full-sized ½-ton pickup was available with four full-sized doors. Previously, crew cabs were only available on ¾-ton-and-up trucks. New for 2005 was a gas/electric hybrid version of the Escape. Its drivetrain coupled a four-cylinder engine with an electric motor, and the vehicle would run on a combination of the two or either power source depending on conditions. Also reducing Ford's impact on the earth in 2005, the thirsty Excursion was dropped. In 2010, Ford brought its compact European Transit Connect van to North America. A high roof allowed the van impressive cargo capacity for its size. Most Transit Connects were sold in cargo van form, but it was also available with two rows of seating. Also in 2010, F-150 added an off-road-performance Raptor model, available with a 400-horsepower 6.2-liter V-8 engine.

Top: The 2000 Ford Explorer continued to be offered in four-door form (shown) or as the less popular two-door Explorer Sport. **Above:** The 2000 Excursion dwarfed its closest rival, the Chevrolet Suburban, by being longer, wider, taller, and nearly a ton heavier. **Right:** F-150 was redesigned for 2004. The popular four-door SuperCrew (shown) returned, but all body styles had four doors—even the regular cab, which had two small "quarter doors" in the back to access to storage space behind the front seat.

Top left: The 2005 Escape Hybrid was Ford's first hybrid SUV. Fuel economy was impressive, with EPA ratings of 33 mpg city and 29 highway. **Top right:** By 2009, E-Series had been America's most popular full-sized van for 29 years. **Above:** The front-drive 2010 Transit Connect van was powered by a 136-hp, 2.0-liter four-cylinder engine with a four-speed automatic transmission. **Left:** The 2010 F-150 Raptor had modified suspension and a significantly wider track for high-speed off roading.

Index